Sir Tom Cowie
A True Entrepreneur

A Biography by Denise Robertson

**University of
Sunderland Press**

SIR TOM COWIE

© Denise Robertson

ISBN 1 873757 84 0

First published 2004

Cover Design by Tim Murphy Creative Solutions
Cover Photography by Mike Smith Photography
Copy-Editors Felicity Hepburn and Heather Russell
Typesetting Moira Page

Published in Great Britain by
The University of Sunderland Press
in association with Business Education Publishers Limited
The Teleport
Doxford International
Sunderland SR3 3XD
Tel: 0191 5252410   Fax: 0191 5201815

British Cataloguing-in-Publications Data
A catalogue record for this book is available from the British Library.

Printed in Great Britain by the Alden Group, Oxford.

To the University of Sunderland

SIR TOM COWIE

Acknowledgements

I'd like to express my gratitude to all the people who have helped in the writing of this book, especially Edgar Turner for his glimpses of the past, and Maureen Bryant for her unfailing patience and efficiency.

SIR TOM COWIE

Contents

Author Biography

Denise Robertson was born in Sunderland and still lives nearby. Her first novel won the Constable Fiction Trophy and her first television play the BBC Review Play Award. She has worked in television since 1984, now appearing regularly on ITV's *This Morning*. As a journalist she writes for both national and regional newspapers. She has written 18 novels, and in 2003 published *How to be a Good Parent*, a guide to bringing up children.

SIR TOM COWIE

Foreword

Ten years ago almost to the day I was flying down to Spain to shoot partridges in La Mancha. I had been told by the organisers to look out for one of the other guests in the BA Lounge at Heathrow.

'How will I know Sir Tom when I see him?' I asked. 'He certainly won't be able to pick me out. The lounge will be full of Smiths.'

'Look for Jack Hawkins. That will be him.' And so it was. We shook hands and he said something that made me laugh, and we didn't stop laughing and talking for the next three days.

Since then I have come to know Sir Tom really well, and I can find no vice in him. He is shrewd but generous, a hugely accomplished and successful businessman but, at the same time, a modest and down to earth gentleman with marvellous old fashioned manners. He has a dry and delightful sense of humour, and he can coin a pun with the best of them. He loves sport, and is a great shot. One of his other passions is jazz music, of which he has an encyclopaedic knowledge. He has devoted much of his life to helping others less fortunate than himself. He is a past president of the Sunderland Football Club and is currently Chairman of the Board of Trustees of Sunderland University, where his fundraising efforts for that institution are indefatigable. The proceeds of this book will go to the University.

In the ten years since we first met we have travelled together to Africa and Spain and South America sharing numerous adventures and much fun.

I can thoroughly recommend this biography to you as an important record of a good life lived to the full.

Wilbur Smith

Chapter One

In the Beginning

Sometime in the 1870s, a young sailor named George Cowie came to the port of Sunderland. Still in his early twenties, he had sailed the high seas, meeting up with Buffalo Bill when he jumped ship in America. Now, though, he had had his fill of adventures and wanted to settle down. Why he chose Sunderland instead of the more prosperous city of Newcastle, 12 miles up the coast, we will never know. What is certain is that, if he had not chosen Sunderland, the commercial face of that city in the twenty-first century would be very different. Sunderland may have offered a convenient hiding-place, for there were rumours of a wife who took to drink and of a child left behind in Scotland. Perhaps he chose the town because he fell in love, for we do know that on 29 January 1884 he married Catherine Ann Sait, at the Parish Church of St Hilda in South Shields, with his father listed as a jeweller and Catherine's father described as a seaman. George was 27 years old and Catherine 22. The couple set up home at 61/2 North Moor Street, in Sunderland's East End. George tried his hand at many trades, eventually joining the fire brigade, where he defended his fellow workers' rights with such passion that he was once sent to jail for trade union activities. Eventually he became a ferryman, taking passengers across the River Wear at a halfpenny a time.

At that time Sunderland, the name of which derives from the 'sundered land', was divided into two halves: to the north lay the working-class community of Monkwearmouth and the semi-rural area of Fulwell; to the south were the commercial heart of the town and the teeming alleys of the East End. Far enough away for comfort lay the leafy suburbs where shipbuilders and merchants lived in some splendour. St George's Square, for instance, its gardens protected by massive gates, admitted carriages only and excluded 'tradesmen, hawkers, dogs or children playing rough games'.

There were plenty of rough games in the East End— and not just for children. The actor Henry Irving, playing at the Lyceum Theatre in 1856, admired the 'stupendous' Wear Bridge but deplored 'the tail of High Street, inhabited by the lowest class of people, principally mechanics and sailors, and from which branch off, to the right and to the left, many very narrow passages or alleys, all presenting, at the time of my visit, the very sink of gloom and filth'. Thirty years later the area still boasted

144 public houses, a large number of pawnshops and 57 brothels.

In a town accepted by Victorians as the greatest shipbuilding port in the world, there were two breeds—those who lived in squalor and those who earned their money in the town and escaped to its outskirts to rear their families. However, as the nineteenth century drew to a close, things were improving. Streets of cottages were appearing in such places as Millfield to bridge the gap between rich and poor. They were small, terraced houses, often single-storey, designed to be homes for skilled workmen and the lower-middle classes. Prosperity was filtering down, and those who could do so were improving their lot.

Escape from the East End might be beyond them, but George and Catherine Cowie were determined that their offspring would have a good upbringing. George turned his hand to anything that brought in extra cash, and Catherine sold toys door-to-door from a wicker basket. There were eight children in all: George, Jim, Tom, Jack, Catherine, Alice, Hannah and Margaret (who was nicknamed 'Clon' because she was born at the time of the Klondyke Gold Rush). None of them went hungry; they were clothed and shod and generally happy. Today, their grandchildren still remember George and Catherine as loving grandparents.

George had always been fascinated by bicycles. With the growth of the railways and the gradual demise of the horse-drawn carriage, the bicycle was becoming the favoured means of transport of the ordinary man and woman.

Leonardo da Vinci had sketched something akin to the modern bicycle in 1490. Three hundred years later, the French invented a wheeled machine that was propelled by pushing the feet against the ground; however, it was a Scottish blacksmith named Macmillan who, in 1839, invented the first bicycle with pedals. George watched the bicycle evolve rapidly as the nineteenth century drew to a close. Spoked wheels, solid rubber tyres, lever-operated gears – one improvement followed another. In 1896 a 'bike' cost the average wage for three months; by 1909, one could be bought for less than one month's wages.

George built and restored bicycles (at first with rope tyres), which he then hired out for a halfpenny an hour. He liked to ride them, too, and—well into his seventies—thought nothing of cycling from Sunderland to Edinburgh. Did he visit a first wife and son there? We will never know. Rumour has it that, when his jeweller father died, George could not claim his inheritance because he had allowed his family to believe him lost at sea.

Of all his children, George was closest to Tom, his third child, probably because they shared a passion for wheels, although 'push-bikes' were too tame for Tom, who favoured motor bikes. Father and son were close in everything except their political leanings. Where George was a true Socialist, Tom (who had been christened Thomas Stephenson Knowles Cowie), had only one ambition—to build a thriving business and control his own destiny. The leap from child of North Moor Street to entrepreneur could not be managed in one bound, so he took up an apprenticeship at a Sunderland shipyard and, at the comparatively young age of 19, he married Florence Russell. Florence was one of four sisters, the children of Jack and Emma Russell. Jack had driven a horse-drawn cab and never lost his love of horses. Emma was a gentle, quietly spoken woman who lived for her children and grandchildren. To them she became 'Little Grandma', while jolly, boisterous Catherine was 'Big Grandma'.

Tom and Florence lived with Tom's parents for a while and then set up home in 13 Trimdon Street West, in Sunderland. Their happiness was marred by the death of their first two children in infancy, probably from pneumonia, but in 1922 a son was born, a lusty baby who had inherited the Cowie fair good looks and was christened Thomas. As he grew, Tom Junior liked nothing better than to visit his grandparents in North Moor Street. Even the sharp smell from the public urinal on the corner did not deter him. He revelled in tales of 'derring-do' from Grandfather George, and Big Grandma could be relied on to produce sweeties. Catherine was, by then, a stout, happy woman who loved her gin and kept both purse and snuffbox in her ample bosom. Her favourite treat was a visit to the Gaiety Cinema in the West End, where she was in great demand because she could read out the captions adorning the silent films to those around her who could not read.

George scoured rubbish dumps for discarded car seats, made from high-quality leather. He would strip and clean this leather and use a sewing machine to make purses and handbags for the 27 grandchildren he subsequently acquired. Catherine was fond of making 'clippy' mats—colourful confections of strips of cloth woven into hard-wearing floor coverings. Occasionally, she would take a fancy to a garment some visitor was wearing and ask that it be given to her when outworn, so that she could make clippings from it. If the garment was black, all the better, for her mats always had a black border.

In 1927 a girl, christened Emma after 'Little Grandma', was born to Tom and Florence and the family's future seemed set fair. In 1929 they moved up in the world, to a single-storey, terraced cottage—5 Westbury Street, a house with a front door opening directly onto the pavement—in the respectable Millfield area of Sunderland. Careful with money, they lived better than many of their neighbours, and each summer a holiday was spent under canvas on a farm at Whitburn, a few miles north of Sunderland.

Tom Senior joined them after work each day with his motor bike and side-car and, at only eight or nine years of age, young Tom was allowed to ride the motor-bike around the field. The boy was a Cowie in temperament as well as looks, with the same passion for mobility; if Florence had sometimes to cover her eyes for fear her dearly loved son would break his neck, she knew better than to deny his fun.

But the tide of prosperity that had carried Sunderland from one century into another was ebbing. It was 1931; the world economy was collapsing into the worst depression in history, and demand for shipbuilding plummeted, taking Tom Cowie's job with it. It was now that the entrepreneur in him came into its own. He tried his hand at selling insurance; found and worked a little drift mine, shipping its coal from the Wear; and then turned his hobby of repairing motor bikes into an occupation. He went to work for a man called Ken Blakey, who had premises in Brougham Street, off Crowtree Road; Tom started as a mechanic but rapidly came to share in the management of the business.

The idea of bolting small engines onto cycle frames had come with the turn of the century. By 1907, the winner of a Tourist Trophy (TT) race on the Isle of Man was averaging 38.23 mph over 10 laps. By the time that Tom Cowie went into business you could buy an 'Unapproachable' (a Norton model) for £49 15s 0d and, if you were a family man, it came complete with side-car. Prices would remain largely unaltered throughout the thirties, putting transport within the reach of the working class. Blakey's had no shortage of customers, and Tom Cowie could hardly believe his luck in having found a lucrative form of employment that allowed him to indulge his passion for speed.

He might have stayed at Blakey's, building up that business, if fate had not taken a hand. A motor bike that was being kick-started, backfired and then burst into flames. No lives were lost but the petrol stored on the premises ensured that a dozen motor bikes and the building itself were burned to cinders. Tom Cowie took his share of the insurance money and set about restoring his fortunes. To Florence's initial horror he announced the birth of a new business—T. Cowie & Son—located at 5 Westbury Street. At first, this involved only the tiny backyard, where a workshop and store were hastily created in which to repair and sell motor bikes; however, as the business prospered, Tom commandeered the back bedroom and knocked out the wall that separated it from the yard. Florence may not have been a natural entrepreneur but she was a good wife: her job was to keep a happy home and, if business nibbled at the edges of that home, she would find a way to cope. Besides, her hands were full dealing with two boisterous children. Young Tom was a lively lad and she needed to keep an eye on him. A good 'northern wife', she tended the home and trusted her man to provide.

Chapter Two

Young Tom

As Tom Cowie Senior struggled to build his business, the industrial climate was not in his favour. Between the wars, Sunderland was to go through a period of considerable growth but also of great hardship. The town extended its boundaries; the development of both private and public housing transformed living conditions for many; nevertheless, however much civic leaders strove to improve things, conditions beyond their control had a negative effect.

Throughout the centuries, Sunderland's prosperity had been built around the building and repairing of ships, industries which employed about a third of the adult population at one time. However, from the boom time at the end of the First World War there was a steady decline in world trade. Once the international economy began to recover, shipyards in Europe, Japan and the United States challenged Britain's predominance. In the early 1930s the total number of ships built on the Wear in a year was what might have been built and launched in only 6 months, 20 years earlier. Yard closures became a permanent feature of the town's existence. In 1934, over half of the working population was unemployed. At the outbreak of war, five years later, a quarter of the town's workforce was idle.

To make matters worse, new industries (which used electricity and were therefore not directly reliant on the coalfields), went to the Midlands and the South. The level of deprivation in the town was all too obvious to young Tom. Some of his fellow pupils at St Andrew's Church School in Deptford went without shoes and showed obvious signs of malnutrition. He understood that he was lucky, even privileged, but he enjoyed primary school because he was seen as a bright boy who learned easily.

The idyllic Cowie family life continued through the thirties, but now the bell tent on the Whitburn farm had been replaced by a caravan. There were Cowie cousins galore, 28 in all, which meant that there was always someone of his own age to play with—although nothing could compare with a chance to ride pillion on his father's motor bike. When the family acquired a car, came the thrill of navigating it around a field while his mother sat in the back seat, calmly knitting.

In spite of Sunderland's problems, Tom Cowie's business was prospering, which was due in no small measure to the personal attention he gave to customers. He loved his own motor bike; he wanted others to know the same pleasure. This ethos of customer care would continue. Fifty years later the eyes of Tom Junior, now a Knight of the Realm, would fill with tears when an elderly man accosted him in a hotel lobby to thank him for the pleasure he had received from a motor cycle sold to him by Cowie's more than half a century before.

By 1934 the business was profitable enough for the family to move from the close ranks of Millfield's terraces to Meadow Gardens, a leafy cul-de-sac on the prestigious Queen Alexandra Road. No more brick yard crammed with motor cycles; now there was a lilac tree, a lawn and birdsong. As Florence Cowie pegged out her first washing in the green garden, Adolf Hitler was abolishing the right of appeal in Germany's courts. Three months later the German people swept Hitler back to power with 90 per cent of the vote. Henceforth, the men of Germany's armed forces would swear a 'sacred oath of unconditional obedience'—not to their country but to Hitler personally.

Probably, young Tom gave little thought to what was happening in Europe. He was much more likely to have been fascinated by the gory demise of the American bank robbers Bonnie and Clyde, shot dead in an ambush in Louisiana in that same year. He was definitely more concerned with his new school, the Bede Collegiate School, where he was forced to study English, history, science and French. At his church primary school he had enjoyed lessons, particularly arithmetic, because he could see the purpose of understanding pounds, shillings and pence. Now he was made to learn things which he felt had little relevance to his future. What was the importance of long-dead kings and queens or the usefulness of the language of a country he would never visit? Moreover, how could any lesson be half as fascinating as what was going on in the motor-cycle repair shop, now moved to 1 Matamba Terrace, Millfield?

Edgar Turner, a fellow pupil who later became Tom's lifelong friend and colleague, remembers him as an unexceptional pupil, bright and popular but not noticeably a leader. He did, however, have a nice line in nicknames for masters who hounded him to work harder. The maths master, Mr Berry, was 'Bugger Berry' because he wanted Tom to concentrate on algebra—a sophisticated science that Tom could not apply to the buying and selling of bikes. A good second-hand bike could be bought for a 'tenner', and there were plenty of purchasers. Young Tom watched the business grow and itched to be part of it. In vain his mother pleaded with him to stay on at school and achieve academic glory. Apart from football, which he enjoyed, he didn't give a fig for lessons. How could he, when he knew he was born to the motor trade? Now his single-mindedness was brought to bear on his mother. When he was 15, Florence capitulated: young Tom was allowed to leave school and join his father in the business.

Cowie Senior was as excitable as Florence was unflappable, but he was given to sudden moods of depression and extreme pessimism. The moods went as instantly as they had come, and between them he was wonderful company. He had mastered the mouth-organ, the violin and the accordion to an almost professional degree, and he was a good manager of money, ready to fund business expansion when it was warranted but always keeping something in hand for a sudden emergency. He had two vices—an addiction to the smoking that would eventually kill him and an inability to lose even the simple board-games or table billiards he played with his son. However, he believed in delegating: young Tom was given a cheque-book and allowed to buy and sell on his own initiative. 'Remember when you sign a cheque, it's your money and mine you're parting with', his father said—and left the boy to get on with it.

At this time the British motor cycle industry was booming: BSA, Norton, Sunbeam, Rudge, Ariel, Triumph – the list seemed endless. In 1937 a new Red Panther motor cycle cost £29 17s 6d, with 7s 6d extra if you wanted footrests for a pillion passenger seat (which had once cost you 12s 6d). Other makes were dearer, but petrol cost around 1s 0d a gallon, so transport was within the reach of a working man (whose average wage would be around £3 10s 0d a week). Tom Senior worked long hours, often until 10 or 11 p.m. A Cowie cousin remembers one of Emma's birthday parties in Meadow Gardens and a young guest exclaiming that 'there was a workman looking through the window!' The 'workman' was none other than the master of the house in his work clothes, come home early to join in the fun.

If the threat of war had ever hung over Meadow Gardens, it was dissipated by Chamberlain's return from Munich in the autumn of 1938. The Prime Minister promised 'Peace in our Time'—and, if Czechoslovakia had been sacrificed in the process, that was a far-off and little-known country. For young Tom the world seemed the juiciest of oysters: he had his own motor bike (a gleaming Red Panther), and cousin Alex to accompany him to the TT races. For his seventeenth birthday he would be given a car, a blue Standard Eight coupé, registration number GR 7226 (which, when added together, came to 17); it would become his pride and joy.

His cousins remember young Tom as a kindly figure. He would give them money occasionally (sometimes paying them to go away and give him some peace), and he always had a kind word for them. On one occasion he came to visit a branch of the family in Wolsingham; it was harvest time, and he stripped off his shirt to help with the haymaking. The fair-skinned boy got badly burned and had to be smothered in oil, but his own solution was to mount his bike and roar along the country roads to cool off in the rush of air. When he came back, his cousin Jess was fascinated to see a thousand tiny flies stuck to his bare torso.

Consumed with fervour for his job, he devoured news items concerning the motor trade, but Kristallnacht passed him by. On that night in November 1938, 7,000 Jewish shops were looted in Germany; hundreds of synagogues were burned to the ground and an unknown number of Jews perished. The name 'Kristallnacht' came from the mounds of broken glass that littered the pavements, causing Hermann Goering to remark that 'they should have killed more Jews and broken less glass'. Unknown to young Tom, the course of his life was being quietly but inexorably altered. On 8 December 1938, T. Cowie

Limited was formed, with Tom and Florence as Directors and young Tom as Company Secretary; he was 16 years old. When the accounts for the first year's trading were published, they showed a profit of £42 6s 6d.

By the spring of 1939, Britain and France were pledged to defend Poland if Germany attacked. In Sunderland, air-raid shelters were erected and gas masks handed out; however, as summer dragged on, the preparations for war had an air of unreality. Surely Chamberlain would fly to Munich and once more snatch peace from the jaws of war? It was not to be. Shortly before 6 a.m. on Friday 1 September, German forces crossed into Poland and, two days later, Britain was at war. Young Tom's halcyon summer was at an end.

SIR TOM COWIE

Chapter Three

The Outbreak of War

War was declared on Tom Senior's fortieth birthday. On what should have been a day of celebration, he contemplated a bleak future. As a major shipbuilding centre, Sunderland was sure to be bombed. In addition, every available vehicle would be commandeered for the war effort, and the business he had painstakingly built up over the previous five years would be one of the first casualties of conflict.

Within minutes of the Prime Minister's announcement that Britain was at war, air-raid sirens sounded; however, instead of taking cover, the people of

Sunderland came out of their houses, anxious to discuss the situation with their neighbours. When a policeman remonstrated with one group, a man told him 'We'll take cover when the pubs open'. The 'phoney' war had dragged on for so long that no one could quite believe in the real thing. Eventually, the *Sunderland Echo* would take its readers to task over their nonchalance and remind them that war was not a game.

Ironically, if it had been possible for Tom Senior to sustain the motor-cycle business it would have boomed. Sunderland's workforce, for so long unemployed, was swept into war work, giving men and women undreamed-of wealth. Typically, the elder Cowie spent no time in bemoaning fate. With the ability to adapt that had characterised his working life so far, he decided to go into the one industry that even war could not compromise—the production of food. Inheriting his father's love of the sea, for a long time he had kept a small boat on the river. Now, he bought two fishing boats, seine-netters that could trawl the seas out of Sunderland. Fish, unlike meat, was never rationed, and a hungry populace was willing to pay for it. A fish-and-chip shop in Trimdon Street, with Florence in charge, proved the perfect outlet and, before long, he was presiding over another lucrative business.

As enemy U-boats made deep-sea fishing too dangerous, off-shore fishing came into its own. It was not a trade without difficulties: rough seas were one thing, rough crews another. Life on the trawlers was hard and, when they came ashore, most of the men would make for the nearest pub to blow their hefty wage-packets. Often, Cowie had to press-gang his men back to sea with a mixture of threats and cajolery—but there was no point in threatening the sack, for there were other jobs aplenty. Young Tom had often seen out-of-work men gathering on waste ground near his school to play quoits, hurling the heavy iron rings in an attempt to relieve their boredom; now, no-one was bored, and unemployment was only a memory.

Although, from his early teens, young Tom had been able to strip down and repair a motor bike, suddenly, at 17, he found himself left to manage the final throes of the family motor-cycle business. There were no new motor bikes to be had—and used ones were hard to come by, as owners hung on to machines that they knew could not be replaced. He started to attend Army sales and was able to buy up dozens of discarded machines. These he reconditioned and sprayed in traditional cycle colours, with the help of the two young boys still working in the business. Once on display, the bikes sold like hot cakes—mostly to the Army, who politely requested that the bikes should be sprayed khaki before they were delivered!

Sunderland had been preparing for war since 1935, when the government had instructed local authorities to begin to protect their populations. The Corporation had made ready to deal with 4,000 dead bodies—1,000 to each of the town's four cemeteries. Several schools were earmarked as mortuaries, and a Cleansing and Decontamination Depot was set up at Railway Row, in case of gas attacks. On one day—Saturday 24 September 1938—50,000 people were fitted with gas masks (although, to the alarm of parents, no masks were available for infants).

In 1939, a scheme to provide underground protection against air attack had to be scrapped because, at £500,000, it could not be afforded. Now, as the war advanced, the people of Sunderland had to rely on trench shelters, basements or the steel shelters supplied to individual householders – Anderson shelters for outdoors or Morrison table shelters for inside the home. Air Raid Precautions (ARP) services in the town were excellent: in fact, Sunderland ran a Rescue School for County Durham, and almost 1,400 people—paid staff and volunteers—were ready for air raids when they came, the first raid occurring on 27 June 1940.

Eventually, Sunderland would become the most heavily bombed English town north of Hull, and its compact, highly populated character made it an easy target. People became so familiar with air attack that, in May 1943, the Mayor had to issue a warning to 'raid rubbernecks', who were leaving their shelters to 'watch the fun'—the spectacular action of searchlights and fighter planes above. They were also lulled into a misplaced sense of security by false alarms: of the 247 times that the siren sounded during the war years, more than 200 did not herald immediate danger.

In spite of the raids, the early days of war held a strange excitement for young Tom. Although he could no longer make his annual pilgrimage to the Isle of Man TT races, he still had his friends and girlfriends in plenty. They shared his love of music (mainly jazz in the George Shearing style), and sometimes made their own music with piano, guitar and violin. Years before, Florence had tried to persuade him to take piano lessons but he didn't persevere. 'I wanted to play like Oscar

Peterson in half an hour', he says today. 'When I couldn't, I gave up'.

In their hearts, though, they all knew that soon the partying would cease and somehow that added an edge to their enjoyment. One by one they were called up or went to civilian war work. For Tom, that moment came in November 1942: the shop at 1 Matamba Terrace was closed down, along with a subsidiary branch in Newcastle's Scotswood Road, and he went off to join the RAF, his request to become an army dispatch-rider having been ignored. He applied to be a rear-gunner but failed the eye test, much to his disappointment. If he'd succeeded, the Cowie luck might have run out: the chance of aircrew surviving at all was only 40 per cent; that of surviving unscathed was only 25 per cent.

His first posting was to Padgate, near Manchester, where he was given uniform, hat, boots and utensils. He had never been away from home before, unless on a jaunt with friends; now he was to eat, sleep and live in close proximity to a hundred other men. Instead of Florence's beautifully cooked food, there was poor food slopped onto a plate. 'No use complaining now, son' the sergeant told him, 'the fun is only just beginning'.

For three months he square-bashed, sat in at lectures and was hectored by fearsome NCOs, but the homesickness he had felt at first was elbowed out by the constant round of activity and, by the time that he left Padgate, he had adjusted to his new life. His next posting was to Squire's Gate, outside Blackpool—a great improvement on Padgate: men had digs in boarding houses; the food was reasonable and, at night, the delights of Blackpool beckoned. He danced to the mighty Wurlitzer organ in the Tower Ballroom and, though (like Cinderella), he had to be back by midnight, he enjoyed himself with fellow servicemen, with some of whom he still has contact. By day he studied the aero-engine. Although his knowledge of motor cycles was helpful, the aero-engine was much more sophisticated and he studied hard. 'One tiny mistake', he wrote at the time, 'and it would be curtains for the crew'.

Eventually, he was sent to Haverfordwest, in Pembrokeshire, where he was stationed at the Coastal Command Station. Here he found glorious beaches—Whitesands, Newgate and St David's—places where energetic young engineers on 'push-bikes' could race to their hearts' content. His job was to maintain and repair the engines of the Hudson planes watching over the incoming and outgoing Atlantic convoys, keeping them safe from U-boat wolf-packs. On one occasion he was making certain that an engine was airworthy, when an aircrew member started it up: Tom was blown off the plane onto the hard runway below. The injuries he sustained then, though seeming slight at the time, have dogged him through the years in the form of neck and back pain.

Before long he was on the move again, aboard a train bound for Oban, *en route* for the Hebridean Isle of Tiree. Here accommodation was basic – Nissen huts and few amenities. When weather permitted, he could see Barra in the Outer Hebrides and look past Mull to mainland Argyll. In summer, with the Gulf Stream to warm things up, it was pleasant, but in winter the winds came straight off the Atlantic, from icy Greenland, and Nissen huts were poor protection. A visit to the outside lavatories meant a battle with howling gales and lashing rain, and the hangars where the men worked were open at both ends, making perfect wind-tunnels.

Tom was regularly soaked to the skin, and the small stoves in the Nissen huts gave minimal warmth. In spite of this, he enjoyed his time on Tiree, especially when there was a trip to the local dancehall in the company of the few WAAFs stationed there. On one occasion, not fancying the long, rain-soaked walk home, they 'borrowed' an officer's car parked nearby and drove back to base in comfort. And there was one distinct advantage to being on Tiree: the island was classed as an overseas posting, which meant extra leave. He travelled back to Sunderland on over-crowded, slow-moving trains, wondering all the time what he would find when he got there, for Sunderland was now suffering heavily from enemy bombing.

People, by now accustomed to air raids, were refusing to leave theatres and cinemas to take shelter. Between 1939 and 1945, 267 civilians and 28 ARP personnel were killed in Sunderland and 1,000 were injured. Most of these casualties occurred in May 1943: on two days in that month, German planes used a pattern of concentrated bombing over Sunderland, deploying parachute mines, high-explosive bombs and hundreds of incendiaries. T. W. Greenwell's ship repairers, and the Laing's, Austin's and Thompson's shipyards, took serious punishment, as did British Ropes. A new liberty ship, the *Denewood*, was sunk at her moorings, but it was the town itself that suffered most damage: 153 people were killed, and first-aid posts struggled with a stream of injured people.

The worst incident, caused by a single explosion, took place at a communal shelter in Hendon: 12 people were killed and 10 badly injured. In the aftermath of the raids, more than 5,000 people were homeless. St George's Square, where once 'rough games' had been forbidden, was a scene of carnage as people died, sheltering in the cellars of their gracious homes. As a result of the two May raids, 534 houses were demolished, and almost 20,000 needed extensive repair. For a young man away from home and fond of his family, these were anxious times.

In 1944, Tom was posted to Bircham Newton, near King's Lynn, where he worked on the small airborne lifeboats that dropped survival gear to pilots shot down in the Channel. He worked unsupervised, kitting-up the machines for their airborne drops. It was a relatively boring job, but he was well aware of its importance and took pride in doing it well, until he was posted again, this time to a fighter station north of Folkestone. It was a gathering point for posting abroad and, as he waited there, he felt apprehensive. In those summer days in Sunderland, before the war, he had never even contemplated a foreign holiday; now he was about to step into the unknown.

Chapter Four

India

Tom Cowie spent most of October 1944 at the fighter station. The tide of war was running strongly in favour of the Allies, now, but there was still conflict as Germany struggled to defend what remained of the occupied territories and their own country, breached in the west by American forces. British troops were liberating Greece; the Canadians were in Belgium, and the US drive to reclaim the Pacific Islands was in full swing.

So confident were Allied leaders of eventual victory that a conference to establish a United Nations organisation was already taking place in Washington, but servicemen were less complacent; the memory of the forced surrender at Arnhem on 27 September was too fresh for that. Indeed, the Supreme Allied Commander, Dwight Eisenhower, was warning of the dangers of battle fatigue: 'Psychiatric casualties are as inevitable as gunshot or shrapnel wounds in warfare', his report read, and the young airmen waiting with Tom Cowie for news of their posting could not fail to be apprehensive about what lay ahead.

Tom boarded a converted Dutch troopship, the *Johan van Odenbarveldt* in November 1944, to sail through the Mediterranean and the Suez Canal, bound for India. Conditions aboard the ship were primitive: the men were packed like sardines; the heat soon became oppressive, and privacy of any kind was impossible. They slept in hammocks slung in every conceivable inch of space, leaving no room for any kind of exercise. Taking turns to slop out or help in the galley became not a chore but a welcome diversion. Their reason was saved by a single pack of cards, and gambling on solo whist became a passion. The journey lasted for three weeks, but no one pondered too closely the possibility of attack from the air or from submarines. A year earlier, the Mediterranean had been a dangerous place; now, the battle zone had shifted. So they sweated it out in intolerable conditions that were made bearable only by the companionship of war, and they made jokes about what lay ahead.

It was Tom Cowie's first experience of life outside Britain. He probably felt a degree of excitement at the prospect, but nothing could have prepared him for the moment when he first set foot on foreign soil. Bombay was a huge city—India's financial capital, a leading industrial centre and the premier west-coast port on the sub-continent—but what the young airman saw as he disembarked was a grinding poverty that left him speechless. He had believed that he understood hardship, from his days at St Andrew's school in Sunderland's Millfield: there, children might run barefoot, but they were not malnourished and they had at least the prospect of making something of their lives. The grinding poverty of the street-dwellers of Bombay, who lived out their whole existence from birth to death with no prospect of more than a few annas from a passer-by, was chilling. The heat, the humidity, the sounds and smells of a people without hope hit the 22-year-old hard.

Crammed into a train with ordinary passengers, he set out to travel to Karachi, finding a wry humour in the thought that conditions on the troopship had been palatial by comparison. Flies were a constant, biting menace; the only lavatory was a hole in the floor; there was no food or drink available, except at stations where everyone fought and scrambled for what little was on offer—everyone, that is, except the young airmen, for they had no grasp of the language and no Indian money. The names of the stations became imprinted on his mind as the train rumbled through the stifling heat: Sural, Baroda, Ahmadabad and, at each, a platform littered with maimed people who spent their whole existence begging for alms. He had disapproved of the rigid class structure in his own country; now he was witnessing a caste system beside which that paled into insignificance. At one stop he witnessed a dozen or so well-dressed, articulate, young men throwing stones at two blind beggars—a sight that still disturbs him more than half a century later. When at last they arrived at Karachi and were bounced 25 miles along an unmade road to '320 Maintenance Unit', Drigh Road, the fact that it was in the Sind Desert seemed not to matter; it represented a return to normality.

The Sind is described as 'a desert bordering on an inhospitable coast, where hot and humid winds blow across dunes and plains', but at least there were proper billets, stone-built buildings with sloping roofs and eaves which sheltered the rooms within from the worst of the sun. Having a bed complete with mosquito net seemed luxury, compared with the privations of the journey by ship and train. To be sure, the lavatory was still a hole in the floor, but there was a cool, dark room complete with taps where you could fill a bowl with water and tip it over your head as a primitive shower.

Even as he appreciated the new-found luxuries, however, he was brought up sharp by an attack of the dysentery that was to plague him through his time in India and affect his health for the rest of his life. By the time that he left for home in 1946, his weight would be down to nine-and-a-half stone. Food in the camp was largely inedible; refrigeration was non-existent, and stomach upsets commonplace. If you weren't tied to the lavatories you were coping with 'prickly heat', a daily and nightly ordeal. Luckily, Tom escaped the malaria that afflicted some of his companions, who had to spend weeks in hospital with the dreaded disease which, once caught, never leaves you.

There were compensations, however, and his time in the Sind was more than monsoon and mosquito. The boy who had not expected to visit France stood in awed contemplation of the Taj Mahal and found leave spent in the mountain areas a heavenly break from routine.

Afterwards, he wrote: 'I yearned to escape the heat, dust and flies – and especially the monsoons. Lying in bed with the mosquito tent around you, sweating profusely amid sheets as wet as dishrags, you dream of cool, clean beds. I had two wonderful sightseeing spells of leave, which have left me with the most magnificent and enduring memories to counteract the less-palatable ones'.

He tended to build up his leave into periods of about a month. On one occasion, he travelled by train for hours through the Sind Desert to the United Provinces, passing through Jodhpur, Jaipur and Delhi, waking up to the glorious sight of grass, trees and luxuriant greenery. Approaching Naini Tal, the train climbed gradually up into the hills to an area where there was amazing wildlife and a beautiful lake surrounded by tiny villages; for the young airman, this was a magical moment.

It came as no surprise to him to learn that from March to October, when the monsoon is at its height, the families of the British Raj had moved up into the Himalayan foothills to escape the stifling heat. For at least six weeks the whole United Provinces administration would move to Naini Tal's Government House, an impressive building visible from all the surrounding hills. 'The serenity of my surroundings, the blessed coolness of the evenings, were simple luxuries of sensation more vivid than I had previously imagined possible. Also during that leave I viewed the Taj Mahal, an incomparable marble monument to eternal love'.

Back at Drigh Road, there was another opportunity to relax: an American depot was only five miles up the road, and a regular exchange of social visits developed.

The GIs were friendly, outgoing and helpful to their Allied 'poor relations': they organised beach parties and laid on the transport. Glimpses into the US quartermasters' stores were a revelation: discarded food rations from their troops in the trenches provided the British airmen with the best food they'd had in ages – meat, biscuits, chocolate. Discards they may have been, but to hungry young servicemen they tasted like manna from Heaven.

Tom was also appreciative of the native servants, who did their best to make life on the camp tolerable. He paid a 'dhobi wallah' to wash and starch his shirts, and would occasionally escape to Karachi for a decent meal, where he enjoyed the company of Indians and the Burmese refugees who had settled there. Karachi was a huge city and one of the busiest ports on the Arabian Sea, both for industry and fishing. Nowadays, over four-fifths of modern Pakistan's oil requirements enter through that port, as do pig-iron and scrap for its steel trade; in addition, ships are built and cars assembled. But even then it was large, bustling and noisy to Tom's sheltered Western eyes and ears.

During the monsoon period, from June to September, his dysentery seemed worst. The weather was always hot—up to the mid-70s Fahrenheit in January alone and about 20°F higher in June—but at the height of the monsoon it could climb a further 20 degrees. The humidity was indescribable, and the rain, when it came, could drench a man to the skin in seconds. At 3 o'clock in the morning, mid-monsoon, the ghastly hole in the ground seemed an Olympic sprint distance away, with dysentery sapping the little strength Tom had left. The outward journey possessed the dash of desperation, but the return stagger had no shred of dignity or co-ordination. Amazingly, he didn't let it dampen his spirits and, when the dysentery retreated, he enjoyed life. There were tennis courts and a football pitch at the base, while the RAF had commandeered a little island just off the coast near Muripur for rest and recreation. He received two promotions – Aircraftsman 2nd Class (AC2) to Aircraftsman 1st Class (AC1) and then on to Leading Aircraftsman—but status was his least concern: he wanted the war to end and, if playing his part brought that about, he would be satisfied.

The men at 320 Maintenance Unit were conscripts, the NCOs being the regulars. The officers were mainly ex-civilians—reasonable men, able, intelligent, and prepared to talk even to lower ranks. As far as Tom could see, if anyone gave the men grief, it was the Flight Sergeants: to them, airmen seemed little more than a nuisance they had to endure. In contrast to the situation in fighter-dromes, little contact existed with aircrews: 320 MU was what its name implied—a unit for maintenance of aircraft, which serviced and repaired planes for the whole of the South-East Asian war zone.

One of Tom Cowie's abiding memories of his time in India was Lord Mountbatten's visit. 'We all congregated together to listen to him giving us a pep talk, and I must say he was very good at it. All in all, I found him a very knowledgeable and inspiring man. Our own RAF Commander-in-Chief, Air Chief Marshal Parke, and his fellow High Command, seemed distant and remote figures, but Mountbatten was like Slim or Monty – there, visible and accessible to his men'.

Tom had been at Drigh Road for a few months when the Warrant Officer announced, 'I want somebody to come into the office and sort things out'. So Tom found himself amid a constant stream of incoming modifications to specifications, all of which had to be sorted out and attached to the relevant paperwork. Day after day, he could be found sticking pieces of paper onto other pieces of paper – not the most exciting of war postings, but amongst the safest. He wrote as often as he could to his parents and to his sister Emma: totally different in temperament, brother and sister got on very well. Emma had enjoyed her schooldays; she could speak several languages with ease, and was now studying at RADA. In his letters to Emma he poured out his longing to get home and start life anew. He told her, too, of camp entertainment—shows that the men produced themselves to lighten the monotony.

Victory in Europe was a massive boost, but to men serving in Asia it did not present the immediate prospect of a return home. The Japanese were renowned for their opposition to surrender: if they obeyed their code of honour and fought to the last man, the war in Asia could drag on for years.

The men could see progress: Burma was recaptured within days of Hitler's suicide, and the Australians were retaking the Dutch East Indies. However, in Okinawa, General Ushijima's counter-attack and kamikaze raids had sunk 17 US ships, with a loss of 682 lives. News of dancing on British streets as Germany surrendered gave them the relief of knowing their families were safe, but their hopes were pinned on the massive aerial bombardment of the Japanese mainland that was now taking place. In fact, the bombing of Japan only increased kamikaze raids, as young Japanese flocked to die for their Emperor. Then, on 6 August, the thriving city of Hiroshima was wasted by an atomic bomb: birds burned up in mid-air; skin peeled from people's bodies as they burned to cinders where they stood. It took a second bomb, three days later, on the city of Nagasaki, before Japan bowed to the inevitable and surrendered.

Initial euphoria soon evaporated in a longing to get home. Where once Tom Cowie had thought of nothing but winning a just war, he now thought of the interruption to his ambitions and the time that he was wasting in a foreign land. He was not the only one who was suffering from frustration and yearning to escape the dust and flies: men who had been happy enough to serve their country were now being asked to service civilian aircraft, in addition to RAF machines, as civil air flights resumed. There was no mention of demobilisation, but there were disturbing rumours that large liners such as the *Queen Mary* were being used to ship GI brides to the United States, whereas airmen were being told that 'shortage of shipping' was the reason for them not being sent home. The real reason had more to do with the British Government's desire to keep a military presence in India in case of civil unrest: they had been anticipating this for some time; they had not bargained for unrest among their own forces.

At various stations, including Drigh Road, men refused to turn out on parade. Some commanders acted with tact and discretion; others did not. One group captain rounded up those he considered to be ringleaders and announced that he would execute them one by one unless the strike ended immediately. The men capitulated, and he then ordered hundreds of airmen to parade under a blazing sun in their heavy, winter, blue uniforms. It was deliberately designed to break their spirit. One aircrew member (a Jewish man named Norris Cymbalist, with a passion for fair play) was subjected to a court martial and sentenced to 10 years' hard labour. His comrades were outraged, and showed it. What had begun as a rash of minor protests was turning into a full-scale mutiny because of governmental folly and the ineptitude of senior officers. In the House of Commons on 29 January 1946, Prime Minister Atlee stated that 'incidents' had occurred at 12 stations (the Air Ministry's figure was 22).

For Tom Cowie it was a confusing time. 'It was general knowledge in the canteen about the Drigh Road strike call. On January 17, after dark at 9 o'clock, about 1,000 airmen congregated on the football pitch. The reason given was the anger felt at men being ordered to parade in the midday sun in heavy, wool uniforms. I avoided any involvement, for no way was I prepared to do anything to blot my own copybook. Many attended to hear what was proposed, but remained highly nervous in thought and demeanour. Mutiny in the armed forces was not something to be taken lightly. Not only did I not attend, I wasn't even prepared to ask anyone whether they were going or had been. I was determined to keep myself to myself'.

He had sympathy for what was being said and done, especially for men with families who had been away from home for four or five years. The war was over and they couldn't understand why there was a delay. Things might have been better if they'd been given a specific date to focus on, but that wouldn't have fitted the hidden political agenda. News of the protest spread like wildfire to the other bases and the strikes mushroomed, the names of bases on strike being painted on the sides of the aircraft flying the transporter routes: 'Cawnpore Out'; 'Singapore Out', ran the stark messages. At some bases there was talk of men not wanting to be the 'tools of imperialist policy', but Tom can't remember such views being put forward and he certainly had no inkling of governmental concerns or plans for meeting foreign-policy commitments.

'What we did notice was the change in the attitude of the local people as the months went by. A sullen, non-cooperative antagonism prevailed on the streets of Karachi; sometimes they deliberately blocked our way on the pavements. The Indian servants on base were, by contrast, very good, and friendliness persisted; they earned a steady wage, and we slipped their children the odd bar of chocolate when we could. Essentially, the tide towards nationalism and independence was unstoppable, and we had no desire to be around when the balloon went up'.

Sections of the Royal Indian Air Force and Indian Navy made similar protests to their British counterparts. British troops fired on Indian civilians in the streets. RAF bombers were used to intimidate them, angering many airmen. Much of the information was sketchy, but was passed via the radio stations, so those in Signals were more in the know but most of the men were well-and-truly in the dark. 'Certainly, the fates of such as Arthur Attwood, who was based at Drigh Road itself, or Jimmy

Stone and Mick Noble, were unknown to us. Only the name of Norris Cymbalist at the Singapore base seemed to figure in the headlines—the focus for a campaign. We knew nothing of petitions back home to the new Labour Government or the progress of his trial and subsequent treatment. The feedback was deliberately low-key, and we just waited and made the best of things'.

The Royal Indian Navy now rebelled: 3,000 ratings mutinied in Bombay, many of whom carried flags of the Indian National Congress or the Muslim League. They even trained the ships' guns on the city and threatened bombardment. The RAF was ordered to prepare to sink the ships, and four days of rioting in the city ensued. There was considerable loss of life at Karachi, where the army commander ordered the use of artillery against the mutineers. The Viceroy of India, General Wavell, held the RAF to blame for the unrest, saying that they 'had been allowed to get away with mutiny', but this was palpably untrue: India was getting ready to erupt and needed no encouragement from the RAF.

The government decided that the situation had to be defused: RAF demobilisation was speeded up and, within a few months, an extra 100,000 RAF men were released. Nevertheless, it would be November 1946 before Tom Cowie could pack his kitbag and head for home. As for the people of Britain, they knew little or nothing of unrest in the Service, still less of mutiny; it would be half a century before all the facts were revealed.

Chapter Five

Homecoming

Tom Cowie returned to a town triumphant but battered. Sunderland was one of the most densely populated boroughs in the country: in addition to repairing or replacing the thousands of houses destroyed by bombing, it was obvious that the town would have to expand into the relatively open spaces of Ryhope, Silksworth and Castletown if men and women returning from the forces were to be adequately housed.

Everywhere, or so it seemed, there were bomb-sites: gaping holes in terraced streets; a huge hole where the once-thriving Binns' stores had stood; fenced-off areas around the river—all of them covered in the rosebay willow-herb that seemed to thrive on scenes of destruction, and each one crying out for rebuilding.

To young Tom, however, the town had never looked more appealing. Servicemen returning from Europe might contrast the crowded dwellings of their home town with the superior housing they had seen in Holland and Belgium; to Tom Cowie, still horrified by the poverty he had seen in India, Sunderland seemed almost Utopian. But life in Britain in 1946 was far from Utopian: the economy was exhausted by the war effort and weakened by Truman's abrupt termination of Lend-Lease. In addition, the country had huge imperial and other overseas commitments and, although workers were earning much more than before the war (almost 80 per cent more than in 1938), there was little for them to buy. Food rationing had become stricter; a tidal wave of divorce had engulfed the nation; thousands of couples were still squatting in disused service accommodation, and house-building was merely nibbling at the edges of a huge problem.

Tom Cowie, safely back home in Meadow Gardens, with a mother overjoyed at having her son to pamper once again, cared little for these problems: the war was over; he was home again, and soon he would resume the role of a working man. Beside these contentments, world problems seemed inconsequential.

At first, he was happy to enjoy the simple everyday things he had missed—catching up on events, going to the pictures, dating girls occasionally, but more often enjoying nights out with his old friends. He had received the standard demob issue of a suit, a hat, a shirt, two collars, a tie, a pair of shoes, two pairs of socks, two pairs of underpants, a mackintosh, two studs and a pair of cufflinks, all packed in a cardboard box. In addition, he had received a gratuity of about £100, but his real need was a job. Employment exchanges were awash with men eager for work, and Tom knew that founding his own business was probably his best chance of making a living. But petrol was rationed and new motor bikes non-existent, except to those dealers lucky enough to own a franchise from one of the major manufacturers. As his joy at returning home began to recede, he thought more and more about his future—a future that was not looking rosy.

That Tom Cowie was ambitious is not in doubt; however, in 1946, it is unlikely that his ambition extended further than 'making a good living'. Today, seeing the tycoon striding grouse moors or presiding in the boardroom, it is hard to imagine the young man— thin, and still troubled by dysentery—who walked the streets of Sunderland in those immediate post-war days. He was keen, even desperate, to work—but what could he do?

The answer came after several months of futile job-hunting. George Bridges, the husband of his cousin Eva, had an entitlement to a petrol ration; within weeks of first discussing it, the pair had opened a taxi business, using two old Austin cars that the Cowies had possessed before the war.

For a while, Tom revelled in the success of the new enterprise: he was making money, and he was behind the wheel of a car. However, as the weeks went by, he realised that although the new business was good, it was not good enough. George Bridges ran the office and

Tom did most of the driving, but he could not see great opportunity for expansion and, above all, once he had mastered the art of being a taxi-driver, he found it increasingly boring. Besides, he now had a steady girlfriend, Lillas Hunnam—a pretty, demure, young woman he had met at a dance in the Seaburn Hall soon after his demob. If he was to marry and start a family, he needed to expand.

There was one unexpected bonus to his taxi-driving, however: 'Without doubt, the war-time bane of my life was dysentery. Like an unwanted souvenir, I carried it home and suffered a further two years of discomfort I could well do without. It so happened that, amongst our regular taxi customers, were medical staff moving to and from the Sunderland General Hospital, and one of my most regular passengers was the specialist, Dr Corfield. For me, Dr Corfield was significant in two ways. Firstly, he was an extremely nice person to whom one could chat easily, and our conversations were many as I ferried him to the General. Secondly, he had been many years overseas and the symptoms I carried stood out a mile. Commenting that I looked in less than the peak of fitness, he suggested I come for a thorough examination. About a week later he gave me his verdict: 'In layman's terms, you've got what is called "sand in your system"'. He followed this up with an explanation of how dysentery was bedevilling my innards but would clear up in a couple of years. Knowing that an end was in sight was a relief in itself; the eventual cessation of this unspeakable ailment, sheer bliss!'

With his health improving, Tom was determined to strike out in the business dearest to his heart, the motor-cycle trade. The *Sunderland Echo* and the *Newcastle Journal* now contained the occasional offer of a second-hand bike, and the old shop in Matamba Terrace, Sunderland, still owned by his father, was unused. More importantly, in March 1948 the Government announced that petrol rationing would be eased in June: it would still be on ration but there would be a small allowance for the private motorist. With his father's permission, he took down the boards from the old shop, cleaned up one or two bikes that had been lodged there through the war, and purchased half-a-dozen more that he'd seen advertised. The business opened on the day that petrol became available, 1 June 1948, using the old name of T. Cowie Ltd. His goal was a profit of £40 to £50 a week; however, if a steady job had come up at £20 a week, he would have taken it, for that was a fortune in comparison with the average wage of the time. The first sale was to a William T. Holmes of New Herrington, who paid £65 for a BSA machine.

The myth has grown with the years that Tom Cowie inherited a moderately successful business and turned it into a very successful one. The latter may be true, but the former is not. The firm of T. Cowie Ltd which had existed in the thirties, died in the early years of war. T. S. K. Cowie gave many things to his son – strength of character, a chance to experience management as a boy in the thirties, the loan of premises at Matamba Terrace and a business name. However, he did not hand him an existing business, nor did he wish to participate in the new project, preferring to stay with his trawlers. The business that fluttered to life in Millfield in 1948 and grew into the huge concern that is ARRIVA today, was built by Tom Cowie alone and, in the beginning, by the sweat of his brow.

The expertise that he'd learned from his father in the pre-war years stood him in good stead. He knew that the best time for buying was autumn and winter, when ice and snow made riders reluctant to mount their machines; the best time to sell was spring and summer, when the sun and the lure of the open road became an attraction. At first he worked alone, seven days a week, for Sunday was the best day for finding prospective sellers at home. Rain or shine, he chased every advert personally or bribed friends to buy on his behalf.

His voyages in search of bikes to sell were sometimes hair-raising. 'I was going over to Darlington to pick up some spare parts. Trying to overtake a lorry near Sunderland, I suddenly realised to my horror it was turning right, without any signal being given. I was knocked flying off the bike and suffered two fractured vertebrae amongst the other cuts and bruises. It is a fate which visits many a biker, and I was luckier than most. I didn't ride much after that, and even the TT visits to the Isle of Man became a rare luxury, as work forbade such time off'.

Tom had a loyal helper, a 16-year-old named Alan 'Ginger' Peace. He was there to clean and deliver the bikes, which he did on a motor cycle with an old side-car chassis. The body had been taken off and two very thick planks fixed onto the chassis itself. The bike wheels would fit between these planks, lashed on with rope— unconventional, certainly, but effective. Duly loaded up, Ginger would zoom away, drop off the bikes and ride back. He was out in all weathers, for he was devoted to his employer and to the new business. That is not to say his driving was always of the highest calibre. He also drove for Associated Dairies, and on one infamous occasion was seen scraping a whole line of black 'limos' with his lorry as he hurtled down Sunderland's Hylton Road towards St Mark's Church.

The condition of the motor bikes that Tom purchased varied enormously. Rust was one of the main problems: often, a bike had been in storage languishing neglected indoors or at the back of a garden shed, while its owner was away at war. Others were more lovingly tended, kept in bedrooms or front rooms, greased and wrapped in strips of blanket. Often, they were bought as a selection of parts, and Tom would hold his breath until he had the pieces assembled and knew that he had bought a whole machine. Ginger Peace spent hours polishing these old bikes: a jolly good clean was often all that was required, and they looked truly first class by the time they sat proudly in the showroom. Tom kept prices low and was always willing to make a deal, so the business took off with a vengeance. He employed two apprentices, but he still had to work round the clock: there was more money about, and everyone wanted wheels.

Few people could aspire to a car, but a motor cycle was a dream that could sometimes be realised, especially with the sensible hire-purchase terms that Cowie's could offer. Soon, he could scent success, but with each week his ambitions were expanding. He needed to sell new bikes, but how could he break the grip of long-established business in Sunderland and secure for himself a leading franchise? At the end of his first year in the second-hand trade he made a profit of £5,209 13s 7d. It was better than he could have dreamed of, but now it was not enough.

Chapter Six

In Business at Last

When war came, in September 1939, the entire existing production run of major motor-cycle manufacturers was summarily taken over and civilian models adapted for war service. After the débâcle of Dunkirk, when hundreds of machines had to be abandoned in France, the Luftwaffe singled-out factories that might be involved in war production, anxious to prevent the army re-equipping. In one night alone, they destroyed the Triumph works in Coventry and inflicted damage elsewhere, but the morale of designers and workforces was undamaged. Throughout the duration, they toiled for the war effort and dreamed of peace, when they would be free to explore an expanded and hungry market. The wiser designers knew that the age of lovingly designed individual models was over: post-war demand would be for multiple sales of a few models. They toyed with new and revolutionary designs but, while the war continued, all they could do was dream. The general public had been starved of personal transport and, at the war's end, there would be a mass of young ex-servicemen, accustomed to military transport and unwilling to resort to Shanks's pony as they had done in pre-war days.

In addition, European competitors had been either obliterated during the fighting or forced to surrender their machine tools and equipment as part reparation. During the immediate post-war period, the situation for Britain looked rosy—but only on the surface. During the war she had relied on borrowing, principally from the USA. When Lend-Lease stopped abruptly, Britain was left with a widening trade gap. Stafford Cripps, Labour Chancellor of the Exchequer, demanded 'Export or Bust' from every section of industry. From the motor-cycle industry he wanted 258 per cent of the 1938 export figure, and his deadline was 1948.

As manufacturers obeyed, the trickle of new motor cycles available for the home market dried up. In addition, with the advent of the Cold War in 1947, America (seeing Europe as a bastion against the Soviet Union), started the massive Marshall Aid Programme, mainly to the defeated Axis nations. They reasoned that economically successful countries would be less likely to fall prey to the blandishments of Russia. The shattered motor-cycle industries of Germany and Italy were given brand-new equipment—and so the seeds of the demise of the British motor cycle industry were sown.

To Tom Cowie, however, the problem was much more simple. However many new motor cycles came onto the home market, none would come his way because long-established Sunderland companies such as Dunns, held all the franchises—Matchless, Norton, BSA, Triumph, Ariel and Sunbeam 'Our main competition in Sunderland was Dunn's, an old-established firm originally trading under the name Dunn and Jameson and, coincidentally, first based at the bottom of Westbury Street. During the Second World War, that branch closed; then they re-emerged as Dunn's, centred on the 'Wheatsheaf' on Sunderland's Roker Avenue. They were car distributors for Standard and Triumph, and also held all the major motor-bike franchises. Certainly, we were not seen as rivals—more as the poor relations—which suited Cowie's fine. The company used to buy second-hand bikes from them and, while Dunns' management were all off at football matches on a Saturday afternoon, Cowies' salesmen were busy at our showrooms selling those bikes and building up trade'.

The second-hand business was booming, but profits were small. Tom worked seven days a week and even gave up smoking to free more cash for the business. At times it was necessary to lay in large stocks, ready for the spring-time boom; through the winter, with few people buying, the cash-flow situation scared him. Anxiety brought on digestive troubles horribly reminiscent of his wartime trials, and he couldn't take his troubles home (where he would eventually have a wife and child). The risks he took with stock were an intelligent gamble. He was brave, but he was also cautious, and his father, approving, stepped in with a loan. However, a run of bad winters that seemed to go on for ever was hard to survive. He spent many sleepless nights and developed a thrift that has stayed with him to this day. Like the sovereign he adores, he still has a habit of switching off unnecessary lights.

Whatever the trials of those early years, he never doubted the wisdom of setting up on his own. He enjoyed making decisions and seeing them executed. In 1939, when in business with his father and acting as Company Secretary, he had wearied of laboriously writing letters by hand, and asked for a typewriter. There had followed weeks of discussion and several frowns of disapproval before a typewriter was bought on hire purchase. Now, if equipment was needed, he bought it—gingerly, perhaps, but nevertheless with determination. He also relied heavily on hire-purchase customers, many of whom were miners; they were good payers, and Cowies' profit at the end of November 1950 was £10,671 18s 3d. A year later it had more than doubled, to £23,000. Although there was an ever-increasing market for the product he was selling, there is little doubt that the phenomenal early success that Tom Cowie enjoyed was due to his relentless desire to win—a trait he had inherited from his father. Although he drove himself hard and expected a lot from the tiny workforce that he had gathered, he also showed his workers consideration—which is why they were prepared to work their hearts out for the good of the firm. Chief among them was a fellow ex-RAF man, George Stephinson. George was a born salesman—a larger-than-life personality with a host of virtues. Driving was not one of them: he wrote off at least three cars, but always emerged smiling from the wreckage. When he joined Tom Cowie he was an avid motor-cyclist and saw his new job as something akin to heaven, surrounded as he was by gleaming machines. The two ex-servicemen worked hand in hand. When George was after a second-hand bike and the owner was holding out for more money, he would say 'I'll have to ask my father' and nip back to confer with 'Father'—Tom Cowie, 10 years his junior.

However difficult things were, there was always something to lighten their spirits. 'One chap, to whom I'd recently sold a bike, came back with extremely voluble criticism. Apparently I'd sold him a bike without a gearbox! Somewhat bemused, I humoured him and sought clarification, which seemed to anger him still further. "But when I sold you the bike and you went off down the street, you changed gear, didn't you?" I persisted. "Not that sort of bloody gearbox", he snapped, "The type you have to put yer gear in!". Two people divided by a common language! A few years later, there was the fellow who was running-in a car he'd bought from us. He'd obviously gone over the sensible limit and things had gone wrong. "I've been ever so careful, I've never been out of second gear", he announced smugly, positively preening. Now think about it, 35 miles an hour in second gear! I'll leave you to ponder the nature of the advice I gave him'.

The vast majority of customers were more than satisfied with the service they received and, as a result, Cowie's didn't have to spend a fortune on advertising. You don't have to, when your best achievement is your

satisfied customer—and satisfied customers Cowie's had
aplenty. Offering hire purchase was a huge advantage.
'Often the wives did the paying in, after the husbands
had handed over most of their wage-packets. There were
a few cases of arrears. I guess occasionally the instalment
went on buying an item of lady's clothing or something
for the house or children. Then I'd be faced by irate
husbands swearing blind they had paid. "Well, it's not in
the book", I would counter. I can visualise some very
serious ructions in certain households after my visits.
There was one old gentleman, a Mr Barker, a nice chap
but a dreadful payer, who had bought a little car on hire
purchase. Cowie's were forever writing letters or sending
people round to try to sort something out. He finally
came into the showroom, and a few harsh words were
said about his missing instalments: "Ah well, thee can
have thee bloody car back", he announced in broad
Durham. "There's the key; there's the registration book,"
he went on, slamming each article down on the desk as
his desperation mounted. "There's the insurance and
there's me bloody stomach medicine as well, I'll not need
that any more!" 'Poor old Mr Barker!'

Some of the vehicles Cowie's sold had their own
quirks (especially the bubble-cars and three-wheelers), in
particular one type in which the gear lever had a
disconcerting habit of parting company from the rest of
the vehicle. Combination bike and side-cars were
another source of regular amusement: many customers
refused to heed insistent warnings that riding them
required more comprehensive skills than were needed for
a two-wheeled bike. Off they'd go, secure in their own
infallibility; about 20 yards down the road, a telegraph

post would act like a magnet, drawing them inexorably in its direction and demolishing the side-car.

Tom enjoyed every minute of his working day, and his private life was happy. Moreover, although he had worries, he was beginning to see just how big a business he could build if he could get a toehold in the new motor-bike market. As he cultivated a satisfied clientele and tried to calm the (by now fairly agonising) stomach pains he was enduring, he dreamed of a Cowie empire that might one day encompass the whole of the North East.

SIR TOM COWIE

1924 - Sir Tom aged 2 years 3 months.

Sir Tom's Grandparents George and Catherine on their Golden Wedding Anniversary, 29 January 1934.

Left: Sir Tom's parents Tom and Florence on their Wedding Day, 3 August 1918.
Right above: Sir Tom's mother (standing) and her sister Margaret Ann Brown (Auntie Clon) with her youngest son Gerald Brown on Sir Tom's father's boat 'The Dandy'.
Right below: (from left to right) Lillas Cowie (Sir Tom's first wife), Sir Tom's mother Florence, Sir Tom and his father Thomas Stephenson Knowles Cowie.

Top: In Rome, Sir Tom with Tommy Hughson of J. R. Alexander & Co Ltd, on route to visiting Vespa Scooters in Pisa.
Below left: Sir Tom in India 1942, aged 20.
Below right: Sir Tom's cousins Alex Brown (holding handlebars) and James Kelly (standing at rear) with mechanic Tommy Fearn (left) and a local friendly neighbour.

Top: Taking it easy in Nainital (known as the lake city), India 1943.
Below left: Enjoying Blackpool in the summer of 1941 with an airforce chum and girls they met dancing at Blackpool Tower.
Below right: Sir Tom with best friend and cousin Alex Brown at Alex's brother Joe's wedding September 1947 Bridlington.

Above: Sir Tom's old Headquarters, Matamba Terrace, Millfield, Sunderland.
Below left: Showroom in Albion Place, Sunderland.
Below right: The damage to Sir Tom's Bentley 1960.

Above: Opening of Scotswood Road, Newcastle, 8 December 1959, reputed to be the largest motor cycle showroom in the world; (left to right) Sir Tom, son Andrew, Kaye Don (World Water Speed Record Holder), Claude McCormack (Chairman - Douglas Vespa Scooters).
Below: Sir Tom's father's showroom - Charlton's Garage, High Street, Sunderland, 1959.

Back row: Sir Tom, son Andrew, first wife Lillas, daughter Sarah, (front row - left to right) daughters Elizabeth and Susan.

Chapter Seven

Family Life

Tom Cowie had never been short of girlfriends, but there was something different about Lillas Hunnam, who he met in a dancehall on Sunderland's sea front. She was pretty, but she was also well educated and a prolific reader, who enjoyed her work for an accountant. Before long, Tom was in love. It was a mutual emotion—but, if they married in a town war damaged and desperately short of houses, how could they set up and furnish a home? Britain was still in the grip of shortage. Even when women had coupons to spare, goods were unavailable. The massive balance-of-payments deficit meant that Britain must export and cut back on imports to a hungry nation: all coloured or patterned china went for export and only 'utility'-grade white could be bought at home; furniture was utility only (and almost impossible to come by), and the 'Black Market' in food and hard goods was flourishing as vigorously as ever it had in the war.

As for housing, would-be private builders were up against a wall of restriction. Priority was given to public housing schemes. Permits were needed for everything and, even with a permit, the allocation was inadequate. Timber was restricted to 1.6 standards per house of 1,000 square feet – not enough even for a timber floor. Families, with their worldly possessions stacked on a pram, had marched into disused army camps or unoccupied houses, making do without electricity or gas or even running water in order to get a roof over their heads. More than 46,000 people squatted and, when prosecuted, were treated lightly by the courts. *The Economist* would write 'in a country so law-abiding as Great Britain it is always refreshing when the people take the law into their own hands on an issue on which the spirit of justice, if not its letter, is so eminently on their side'. Thousands of houses were under construction, but demand was still outstripping supply.

When Tom and Lillas eventually married in January 1949, seven months after Tom set up in business, they moved in with Lillas's parents in Coniston Avenue, a quiet street of semi-detached houses near the sea front. A little over a year later, on 17 February 1950, their first child, Andrew, was born. Life with a new baby might have presented difficulties, living with Lillas's parents as they were, but Tom was out most of the time, scouring the area for used motor cycles and selling them as fast as he could lay his hands on them. If he had needed a greater incentive, he had one now—a son to carry on the family name.

The following year he bought his first house, a neat semi-detached in St Chad's Crescent, bought with a mortgage and costing £1,500. It was small, but fronted by a pocket-handkerchief of garden and situated in Herrington, one of the better parts of town. A home of their own was a necessity for, by now, there was a second baby on the way. That baby was a girl, Elizabeth, born on 15 May 1951, and named after the heir to the throne—although the young businessman, hands sometimes grimy from wrestling with a recalcitrant motor bike, could not have dreamed that he would one day walk a grouse moor with his Sovereign or kneel before her to receive the accolade of knighthood.

If circumstances had been different, Tom Cowie might have become a hands-on father, reading bedtime stories or building towers of coloured brick. It was not to be: he worked seven days a week, often for 16 hours a day. That he doted on his children was not in doubt, but he seldom spent time with them. He did take charge on one memorable occasion: the new Queen's coronation ceremony was to be televised. The house in St Chad's Crescent did not boast a TV set, but Lillas had an invitation to watch with friends. The nation came to a standstill for the grand occasion, Cowie's closed, too, and Tom was available to babysit. As *'Vivat Regina'* rang out in the Abbey, Tom changed baby Elizabeth's nappy—the one and only time that he would perform the task for any of his children.

Elizabeth was a beautiful baby, but she cried ceaselessly, and this was hard on a mother who also had a toddler to cope with and a husband working non-stop to provide. Tom longed to spend more time with the children at what was a fascinating stage of their development but, in a way, the new business was a dependent too, requiring most of his time and energy.

'Working most weekends and long hours during the week, squeezing in a family life was difficult. Holidays, when taken, involved a caravan in places like the Lake District, but I've never been a good person for relaxing for any length of time, though the later cruises were an exception. We had two children in quick succession, and my daughter seemed to cry non-stop for the first six months. It all represented a bit of a trial, especially as my health wasn't exactly wonderful with more tummy trouble looming'.

Nevertheless, his work was so interesting, with always something new, people to see, positive action almost every day, that he surmounted his problems. Sales boomed; stock and premises improved; customers multiplied; and he admits to slinking out of the front door of home on many an occasion with a mixture of guilt and relief. At least he was able to provide a fairly high standard of living for his family: it would have been nice to have had more opportunity to play with the children, but today he doesn't know how, or if, he would have wanted to do things differently. What he could have done without was a stomach ailment that was very depressing: in the early 1950s he was diagnosed as having a duodenal ulcer, which left him feeling tired and very depressed. Living on a diet of glasses of milk and boiled fish didn't help matters.

Eventually, after a couple of years of this, Dr Bill Davison (a boyhood friend, home from a spell as a Forces doctor in the Far East), took one look at him and blurted out, 'My God, you look terrible!' He examined Tom and diagnosed acute appendicitis. It must have been grumbling on for ages, and he recommended that Tom go into hospital with all speed. A specialist decided that they couldn't actually operate until the inflammation subsided, however, eventually, Tom was operated on by Mr Sandford, a famous surgeon in Sunderland in his day. 'I felt a lot better after that. The pressures of business combined with illness—no wonder I'd been so low at times! It was wonderful to feel well again'.

Lillas and Tom were to have three more children: Susan, born in 1953; Sarah, born in 1959; and Emma, the baby of the family, born in 1962. And, as the family expanded, so did their living accommodation: in 1956 they left St Chad's Crescent and moved a few hundred yards to 24 Summerhill—a detached house with a large garden and extra bedrooms. The children, as they reached school age, went off to private schools—Andrew to Tunstall and, later, Rugby; the girls to the Church High School and then Malvern Girls' College.

In 1961 they moved 23 miles away to Broadwood Hall, a crumbling mansion set in eight-acre grounds near Lanchester, in the west of Durham, which Tom bought for £6,000. There were walled gardens and views to delight the eye, but dry rot had taken possession; it was lit by oil-lamps, and it would have needed a further

£6,000 to make it habitable. With the speed that had always typified his actions in business, Tom had had it razed to the ground and replaced by a 16-roomed mansion with 'all mod cons'. The man whose boyhood room had been an attic with a skylight was going up in the world, and taking his family with him.

Chapter Eight

Expansion

By 1952, business was so good that Tom Cowie felt able to expand. He opened a branch in Newcastle's Scotswood Road and another in Sunderland's Hylton Road. To his relief, business at both new branches was excellent from the start and, as the Cowie workforce increased, Tom recruited James Barber as Company Secretary. Barber was an accountant, brought in to streamline the company's rapidly expanding financial and accounting systems; in fact, he found a sensible system already in place and ticking-over smoothly. Tom had seen his father's pre-war credit operation and knew that, properly run, it could be lucrative and lead to a higher turnover. Cowie's specialised in large-deposit/shorter-repayment deals, and favoured low-risk customers. Where other firms simply went for sales, Cowie's wanted sound customers who would return regularly to change their bikes. Where they did take on higher-risk customers, they gave them to HP companies—but they kept the good risks (such as teachers and professionals), as Cowies' own.

Tom Cowie counted himself lucky to have found Jim Barber. 'Jim was a shrewd and able man when it came to figures. Very calm on the surface in any situation, underneath at times he used to seethe. He smoked to excess, which I guess was his way of unwinding. He was popular—indeed, it's my guess that everyone liked him, from the mechanics to the Board, beguiled by his courtesy and genuine concern. A tiny little man, he had a big heart. Jim couldn't drive, never learned, and was driven everywhere. In the early days, when it came to going to meetings, I did all the driving and was always the decision maker, but I consulted with Jim, especially on later take-overs. He'd look through the accounts of the company concerned and give me his measured assessment. We never had any major disagreements. That kind of backing and meticulousness is crucial and beyond price. He was a dapper individual and as bright as a button behind his glasses. Once, at the Caledonian Hotel in Edinburgh, someone in the group got a page-boy to page "Sir James Barber": Jim's face was a picture, he positively preened and took the joke in good part'.

There was a sense of community in Matamba Terrace and Hylton Road, the area around the Cowie base. Nearby was St Mark's Church and, opposite, a tiny garage run by a man called Claude Paddon, which

Cowie's bought and converted for motor-trade use. There was a post office, a big furniture store called Staddon's, a doctor's surgery, a barber's shop, a baker's shop, and many more that fell victim to Cowie expansion. Even a former branch of Barclay's Bank was converted into premises for Broadwood Finance as Cowie's expanded in the 1960s. Ultimately, most of this mixture of houses and small shops was taken over as the need for expansion grew. The different Cowie branches held monthly management meetings where they vied for pride of place as the most lucrative section.

A second motor-cycle showroom was opened in St Mary's Place in Newcastle. Another, in Gilesgate in Durham, followed; however, expansion was hampered by Cowies' inability to secure main dealerships. They had been able to pick up a few minor dealerships, such as Francis and Barnett, but the major ones stayed firmly in the hands of long-established businesses. The manufacturers had long associations with such firms as Dunn's; they were not about to jeopardise those relationships to please a newcomer whose bubble might burst as quickly as it had been inflated.

The reign of the British manufacturers, for so long rulers of the international motor-cycle market, was soon to be challenged, however: Japan was gearing up to make an impact on the mass market, and Italy had produced the scooter. Vespas and Lambrettas became the transport of a younger generation that now had money in its pocket. As this foreign invasion gathered momentum, manufacturers were soon happy to press their wares upon the young entrepreneur. By May 1956, Tom Cowie was Vespa's largest distributor in Britain, and he was invited to visit the Vespa factory in Pisa. He was deeply impressed with all that he saw there: without doubt, the Italians were producing a superior product, allied to a more open-minded attitude to research and development. Styling, combined with quality at a reasonable price, was producing a useful runabout for all ages and walks of life. The fuel economy of the Vespa was attractive to the British market, and the film *La Dolce Vita* added a degree of glamour to the machine—glamour being that 'X factor' that governs public taste. The streamlined Vespa production line confirmed Tom Cowie's suspicions that the British motor-cycle industry was losing its grip but, with 100 motor cycles being sold each Saturday from the Scotswood branch alone, he could not envisage getting out of the market—at least, not yet. Nevertheless, he could see that the sleek Italian product would eventually outstrip its bulky British rival.

Tom was becoming adept at marketing. His adverts for 'Cowie! Cowie! Cowie!' soon became both popular and emulated. He remembers, with affection, the small greengrocer who traded near Cowies' Sunderland showroom and began to advertise 'Apples! Apples! Apples!' But it made no difference: soon, an expanding Cowie's had gobbled up that particular trader, as it did many more in the area. Nevertheless, expansion by degrees was not enough.

Too many departments of the booming business were housed in odd corners of Sunderland. This scattered empire was not efficient enough for Tom's standard, and he conceived a new ambition—to build the largest motor-cycle showroom in the world. He began to buy up property in the Scotswood Road in Newcastle, an entire street of 40 houses and two pubs.

Acquisition of the land took some considerable time, although cash was no longer a problem. Business was booming and the bank ready to accommodate a successful young entrepreneur who seemed determined to gobble up his neighbourhood. The war and general neglect had combined to render the area derelict, and each property purchased was a piece of the jigsaw. A one-man operation for repairing lawnmowers, operating from a Nissen hut, occupied the last piece, and the owner (knowing the strength of his position), held out for an exorbitant sum. Tom Cowie was heard to remark that he had just acquired the most expensive Nissen hut in the Western World.

Nor was the start of the mammoth task of construction any easier: the huge crane hired for the job sank six feet into the ground as a result of former underground mineworkings. Nevertheless, work continued and the massive showroom took shape. On 8 December 1959, the *Evening Chronicle* noted: 'Today I saw more scooters, motor cycles and three-wheelers under one roof than I have seen in my life or indeed can be equalled anywhere in Great Britain'. Of the machines on display, 1,500 of them were new, with second-hand models ranging from a 600 cc machine costing £284 to a moped for 45 guineas. When motor-racing ace Graham Hill performed the opening-ceremony another Cowie dream had been realised.

SIR TOM COWIE

Chapter Nine

Bereavement

As the business expanded, with new showrooms seeming to spring up everywhere, the established businessmen of Sunderland looked askance. They could not dislike Tom—his personality precluded that—but they could disapprove of someone who was apparently throwing caution to the winds and doubling his business in size each year. If they had known how cautious Tom actually was—how carefully he planned each move—they might not have been so quick to label courage as foolhardiness and ambition as arrogance. When he applied for membership of the Sunderland Club he was blackballed, probably by someone who saw him as a puffball businessman, destined to be gone by morning. How wrong they were!

To businessmen who had been prosperous before and during the war but who were now seeing their business decline, Tom Cowie's rapid rise must have been a painful experience. He had acquired a brand-new Bentley—a car he lovingly polished himself—and the sight of it around the town was a constant reminder that, as the old industries faltered, one new entrant upon the scene was doing very well.

In 1960, Cowie's purchased the J. R. Alexander motor-cycle dealerships in Edinburgh and Glasgow. Alexander's combined a Ford main dealership with the distribution of most makes of motor bike throughout Scotland, and their warehouses stocked parts for just about every known make. The company had been founded by the effervescent Jimmy Alexander, a famous name in motor-bike retailing and sport alike. His two brothers were scarcely less flamboyant, one being responsible for driving a Model T Ford to the summit of Ben Nevis as a publicity gimmick to enhance their Ford dealership. As far as Tom Cowie was concerned, Alexander's was a reasonably cheap business to buy. It was well established, with good premises on Lothian Road in Edinburgh right next to the Caledonian Hotel and a mere 10 minutes from the railway station—a prime location. Similar claims could be made for the Glasgow premises, where wonderful characters—such as the Manager, George Gavin—kept things buzzing along.

Cowie's considered that it had made a sound investment—one which merited an outlay of £177,000. Annual profits in excess of £50,000 per annum proved this to be right. Alexanders' management was still rooted in a pre-war style; its owners were ageing, and a lack of liquid assets had forced the sale. As far as members of the Alexander family were concerned it was a very amicable deal, though many of the staff were probably less than happy with an English take-over. Tom Cowie installed a few key personnel. George Stephinson was brought in on the Sales side but most of the staff were kept on, for Tom was interested in modernising while retaining Alexanders' traditional character. The discussions and planning had been long but worthwhile. Few other companies were big enough to have taken them over, so rival bidders had been few and far between, but Tom was still relieved when the deal was finalised.

In time, the motor-cycle division of Alexanders' main competitors, Rossleigh Ltd, was also taken over. Added to that, on the opposite side of Lothian Road, between the Caledonian passenger station and a goods-yard entrance, another lavish Alexander depot took shape. The Cowie Lothian Road showrooms could claim to be easily the most extensive in the whole area. It had taken over the main distribution of Suzuki's range of bikes throughout Scotland, and the 50 cc machines were selling well. Now, Cowies' main competition in motor-bike retailing lay far to the south—with King's of Oxford and the London-based Pride and Clarke—but, as Tom eyed possible acquisitions in the south he suffered a great blow: his father—the man who had been his mentor, his friend, his backer when necessary and his staunchest supporter—died. 'I owed much of my business philosophy to my father. Life is basically about timing, especially business. If your timing is right, you can make millions ... get it wrong and it's oblivion. The

Cowie luck was there but it didn't come without a lot of hard work. I knew and understood my product, and the nature of the beast which was the motor-cycle business. My father had seen to that'.

His father had helped to provide cash to stock up the new business in 1948 and had been paid back within two or three years. That he was proud of his son's achievement is not in doubt, but perhaps there was a twinge of envy at the vast proportions the new business assumed in such a short space of time.

Tom Cowie Senior, as well as operating his seine-netters, had taken over Charlton's, a small garage in High Street in the East End district of Sunderland. It was a used-car concern, doing a fair amount of repairs and general body-shop work. He was still working there when he died. Two such strong characters were bound to clash from time to time, but Tom Cowie had always valued his father's opinion and he felt the loss of this support keenly. T. S. K. Cowie had never openly praised either of his children, but they had never doubted his love for them.

Now, as he struggled to come to terms with his father's death, Tom's friendship with his old school-friend, Edgar Turner, became even more important. Edgar Turner had been his friend at Bede School. When they were both working, Tom would frequently pick up Edgar as he waited at a bus-stop, and whiz him to his place of work, clinging to the back of whichever motor cycle Tom was using at the time. Edgar was a civil engineer and, from time to time, would advise Tom on the structural state of buildings that Cowie's were about to purchase. He was later to be especially helpful over the rebuilding of Broadwood Hall, devising a new water system to replace a supply that was unfit for human consumption. He also advised Tom on the building of the new Scotswood Road showroom—and there was yet another link for, by chance, the two men had become next-door neighbours in Summerhill and their wives were now friends.

In 1962, Tom invited Edgar to join the Cowie staff, and he agreed. Eventually, he became Deputy Chairman and remained with Cowie's until his retirement. Today, the two men remain firm friends and Edgar has a clear view of what contributed to Tom Cowie's success: 'Tom has the virtue of seeing ahead and taking positive action. When he became successful he was envied rather than disliked, but he couldn't have cared less. He has never ingratiated in his life nor sought to curry favour. He always saw a ladder ready for climbing and had the courage to make the ascent. He knew how to pick a team that could keep things ticking in his absence. You never think of your school-friends as doing anything out of the ordinary, but he was the exception. I have never had a cross word with him. His virtues are many ... foresight, determination, charm, courage and ruthlessness in equal measure'.

Tom was equally appreciative of his friend. 'My links with him go way back to childhood; we were at school together. He was "the educated one" who excelled at school and went on to college. In total contrast to myself, he was a gifted mathematician and was to become a civil and structural engineer, after serving in the war as a navigator in the RAF. When we moved from St Chad's Crescent in East Herrington to 24

Summerhill, Edgar was my next-door neighbour. We were good mates, with a lot in common; when he later took notes at Company meetings he had a brain like a filing cabinet—a brilliant man'.

Edgar had worked for the River Wear Commissioners and enjoyed the post-war expansion there. But eventually he grew bored by the predictability of his assignments on Wearside and jumped at the chance to join his friend's expanding business. He was a workaholic who cared little for holidays. Ironically, when the company won a competition for a holiday in Bali, Edgar was chosen. While he was abroad he contracted encephalitis—an inflammation of the brain caused by a virus—and was very ill: indeed, he was never the same again, having lost half his vision, and had to retire early.

There is no doubt that having Edgar Turner's companionship on business trips was balm to Tom in the aftermath of his father's death. Edgar has described the Sunderland of those years as 'the biggest village in the country'. It was dominated by families who had been great before the war but whose firms were mostly approaching the end of their useful lives. The aristocrats of the shipbuilding and mining worlds did not take too kindly to the young ex-serviceman whose expanding business was attracting more and more attention. Tom sensed this and was glad to have Edgar's support.

Together, they visited the Turkish baths in Newcastle after big deals and finished off with a massage and a slap-up meal at the then fashionable Phillip's Fish Restaurant, where Tom was known as a generous tipper. However, two more single-minded men did not exist, and their ambition was to take the firm of Cowie's to the top of its genre. In the wake of the Alexander take-over, profits topped the £200,000 mark, and Tom Cowie looked towards Yorkshire. Eric S. Myers of Bradford was a relatively minor acquisition, but it did come with a Morris retail dealership. Ian Appleyard and his Leeds-based Group had purchased it two years earlier. Tom Cowie knew Ian and the deal was smoothly closed. At one stage, Myers' represented the largest showroom for two-and three-wheelers in the whole West Riding.

By 1961, T. Cowie Ltd had major showrooms in Newcastle, Sunderland, Edinburgh, Glasgow, Bradford, Stockton and Durham, but Tom was beginning to have doubts about the future of the trade in which he was currently so successful. The motor-cycle and scooter booms were over and he found himself increasingly frustrated by the behaviour of the British motor-cycle manufacturers. It was not only their refusal to grant him franchises for new machines that irked him, it was also their assumption that their way of doing business was the only way. They saw no need to change practices that had endured since the industry began, and they were oblivious of the threat from manufacturers abroad, although both the quality and the reliability of the Japanese product were staggering. No preferential treatment was being held out to Cowie's in spite of their huge turnover. In addition, British manufacturers played ostrich-like games, even when told of Tom's serious misgivings: 'Crisis, what crisis?' was the predictable, but tragically arrogant response. 'The bosses at BSA in Birmingham's Smallheath were a case in point. Any reservations we had about the future were patronisingly dismissed. In essence, as far as they could see, any fool could sell their product; their only problem was not being able to make enough. So blinkered, so sad, so self-destructive'. When he informed one manufacturer that he had sold 1,000 of their machines, the patronising response was that their machines sold themselves. It was an attitude that was bound to end in disaster.

Chapter Ten

Team Spirit

Members of the Cowie workforce in those early days have vivid memories of the excitement of that time and the family atmosphere that prevailed. Saturday was always a big event: salesmen would congregate at the end of the day, flourishing their pink and white sales sheets, anxious to see whose bundle was the biggest. The Cowie operation was scattered. One workshop was an old undertaker's premises, where elephants had been kept while appearing at the nearby Empire Theatre. The Hylton Road operation was known as 'the boutiques', because it was a string of small shops, each with a single car in the window. Nevertheless,, there was no doubt that the workforce felt that they were part of a family—a family that was going places. Cowie employees tended to be characters: one was also a qualified embalmer; another, frustrated by the no-smoking rule in the showroom, would appear with smoke issuing from his sleeve from the cigarette he had hidden there. Whatever their eccentricities, the staff were united by affection for a boss who was benevolent as long as he was obeyed but whose orders were seldom petty or without purpose. And, however hard they had to work, the boss worked even harder. Jack Keerie, who worked for Tom Cowie all his working life, tells this story: 'This particular day dawned shrouded in a heavy fall of snow. When I got to work, alarm bells were ringing in head office. At noon a number of VIPs had been scheduled to meet the boss. He had planned to drive from home to head office, a distance of 20 miles, as per his normal routine. Local-radio weather reports warned of blocked roads in the Weardale and Durham area and, by 10 o'clock, no change was imminent. Action was called for! My company vehicle was a Land Rover. It was fuelled up, and with two shovels and a senior apprentice with me, I set off to face the elements. As we neared Lanchester, conditions deteriorated rapidly; snowdrifts blocked the road; and then I saw a tractor approaching with what looked like a passenger perched on the draw bar at the back. As we closed on each other and stopped, I saw the boss dressed in his city clothes (including his briefcase) standing on the tractor draw bar, like a paratrooper ready to jump when the light turned green! We transferred him to the Land Rover for the return journey but the drifting snow had become a nightmare. Bottom gear was required to ram our way forward and in some places it took three attempts to drive our way clear through to reach Durham. The road from Durham to Sunderland was clear but when we reached the office we were told that no trains were running and our visitors were still in London'.

As the business extended into other parts of the country the rivalry between branches became even more intense. None of those workers, happy in their competing, could have envisaged the massive shake-up that lay ahead. On a Saturday, the Scotswood branch would sell a hundred motor cycles. But the boom could not last. The staff could see only the prospect of greater conquests, but they were wrong.

Between 1920 and 1960, British manufacturers had ruled the motor-cycle world. In 1959 more two-wheelers were requested than ever before in Britain and there was a healthy level of export to the United States. But the Japanese were beginning to take over the market and they did it rapidly. Years later, the then Minister of Transport, Tony Benn, would commission an enquiry into how the market for British machines evaporated and went to the Japanese, but by then it would be too late: British manufacturers were psychologically incapable of fighting back. In one factory, rows of finished machines stood idle because the man who applied the finishing touches was 'off sick'. The customers for whom those machines were destined probably grew tired of waiting and bought from the Japanese. In addition, there was a new affluence in Britain: men who would once only have aspired to two wheels now saw four within their reach. Within a very short space of time, the demand for British motor cycles vanished like mist from a window. British manufacturers had spent too long pondering what they wanted to make; the Japanese concentrated on what people wanted to buy. There was a worldwide drop in demand for motor cycles but the British industry was exacerbating its own difficulties.

More and more, Tom Cowie's thoughts were centred on motor cars, but the main dealerships he needed were still denied him. Cowie's were retail dealers under a main dealer in Newcastle for Morris cars, but the old-established main dealers held all the aces: they got a discount on each car they supplied to the small retail dealers. Much earlier, when such manufacturers as Nuffield, Austin or Morris had been experiencing cash-flow problems, the main dealers had bridged the gap and taken the cars. In the fifties it was time to return the favour, and this relationship seemed impossible for a newcomer to break.

As the motor-cycle trade dried up it seemed inevitable that Cowie's would change from two-wheeled to four-wheeled vehicles but, for Tom Cowie, the situation was fraught with difficulty. 'The big worry was how successful Cowie's could be in the motor-car world. We had shown we could sell bikes, and were beginning to make inroads into car retailing, but whereas I had friends and contacts in the motor-cycle arena, when it came to cars, I had a sense of being back to "Tom Who"? So many doors seemed locked in our faces'. Years later, in 1964, on a visit to the British Motor Corporation (BMC), a senior official was dismissive, despite Cowie's increasingly impressive financial track record. The comment 'You know, Mr Cowie, you can't expect people like you to make the sort of progress you have made and for everybody to like you', is forever etched into Tom Cowie's memory.

From then on, Cowie's went exclusively for motor-car dealerships, both retail and the elusive main ones. Norman Howey Ltd of Roker, Sunderland, represented a very old-established dealership—one that had sold Austins from its sea-front premises for many years. In September 1962, Cowie's acquired it. Tom Cowie felt that, if he bought up every available retail dealership for Austin and Morris, they would eventually have to appoint T. Cowie Ltd as the main dealers in Sunderland. 'The attitude I encountered at the Earls Court Motor Show, and latterly at the BMC, continued to sting. I'd been told in no uncertain terms that the North East was minor league and I had a long way to go before achieving premier-league status. Determined to buy main dealerships, I contacted all the main motor-car manufacturers—Ford, Vauxhall, Morris, Austin and the like—but nothing seemed to change'. His problem in the early 1960s was that his name, well known in motor-bike retailing, was relatively unknown in the car trade. Being 'Tom Who?' once again, the north-eastern minnow in a new and larger pond, was a very unsettling position for someone desperate to succeed.

In setting up his business, Tom Cowie had shown courage. Building it up had required tenacity. Now, he was to exhibit the ruthlessness that every successful entrepreneur must possess. The Scotswood Road showroom had been his pride and joy, its ranks of motor bikes a testament to his success. But his antennae told him that the day of the motor cycle had passed. It was not that he had fallen out of love with two-wheeled machines—rather that the motor-cycle industry had fallen away. Its demise can best be illustrated by what happened to that giant of the industry, Birmingham Small Arms Company (BSA). That company had been set up in an age when Britain ruled the world (or much of it), and colonial and imperial expansion required a steady supply of rifles. They prospered through the First World War and then turned their attention first to bicycles and then to motor bikes—the 'good old Beesas'—When in full swing, their Smallheath factory covered 1,142,000 square feet and employed 12 thousand people.

The end of the Second World War saw them with a huge production capacity, and a new 'gentleman's motor cycle' was put into production, using the famous Sunbeam name. Sadly, BSA turned down the chance of building a squat, air-cooled motorcar known as the KDF 'people's car' or, more familiarly, as the Volkswagen! Their advertising slogans were everywhere: 'BSA, the most popular motor cycle in the world'; 'Lead the way on a BSA'; 'Perfect in every port'. But perhaps BSA's best advert was Sir Bernard and Lady Norah Docker. Sir Bernard was Chairman of BSA and the owner of the famous gold-plated 'Docker' Daimler. Norah Docker was an ex-chorus girl with extravagant tastes: 'When other girls would be satisfied with a fur, I always demanded mink. When other girls would be satisfied with a zircon, I'd insist on a diamond. If I asked for champagne it had to be pink'. At least one BSA prototype got the chop because Norah didn't like the colour. She called Smallheath 'a sprawling mass of shabby huts and shacks' and BSA's directors 'a crawling, cringey, slimy lot'. By the time that Sir Bernard was ousted as Chairman, the Dockers had given an excellent imitation of Nero fiddling while Rome burned. The opportunity to introduce badly needed new designs was missed and the cracks that spelled ultimate ruin were beginning to show.

The crash of BSA was a culmination of misunderstandings, too great a reliance on the firm's proud history, and bad decisions. Personal self-esteem and egotism had blinded executives to the true state of affairs, and militancy ruled the workforce. Like the rest of the British motor-cycle industry, BSA had lost the art of building the smaller bike and building it economically. The A10 Golden Flash of the 1940s took weeks to produce; the Rocket Three of the 1960s took six years! Ironically, when bulldozers flattened the site of the once-thriving Smallheath factory, it was turned into a municipal training ground where young motor-cyclists could zoom around on Japanese machines, conducting a bizarre dance of death on the grave of Britain's once-proud cycle industry. It would be years before Smallheath's final demise but, by 1961, the writing was on the wall for anyone with the wit to see it.

Edgar Turner has described Tom Cowie as 'always seeing a ladder he might ascend'. He also had an aptitude for spotting a snake down which he might slide. The Scotswood Road motor-cycle showroom was stocked with a dazzling array of bikes, but customers were becoming scarcer by the minute and Tom knew why: motor bikes were getting dearer and cars cheaper. Parents no longer wanted their offspring to tear around on increasingly high-powered two-wheeled machines. Above all, the working man had aspirations undreamed of when the Cowie business was started. The family saloon was every man's dream: a motor bike and side-car would no longer do.

Chapter Eleven

Turning Point

In 1963, Tom Cowie and his deputy, Jim Barber, visited Japan as guests of the Honda company. The experience was a revelation. 'In 1963 my visit to Honda in Tokyo was an education of the most fundamental kind. No specialist knowledge was needed to read the stark writing on the wall, for both motor-cycle and car manufacturers in Britain. All it needed was a pair of eyes and a bit of imagination. The Japanese were proud of their advances and no wonder'. The Cowie party was courteously ushered around vast mechanised complexes which made Western attitudes seem positively Luddite by comparison. Tom was fascinated but appalled at what all this would inevitably mean for the domestic industries at home. At BSA it was still little wooden trolleys, all piecemeal and small scale; here, the sheer size and efficiency took his breath away. 'The research and development department alone was as big as the whole BSA factory. All was seamless automation: bikes rolled off at a phenomenal pace, were meticulously tested and driven away at a prodigious rate. Here was a devastating combination of speed of production and incredible reliability'.

He knew he was witnessing a quantum leap in business methods and acumen. The bikes had power equal to twice that of their British counterparts, and the one-touch starting mechanism was ease and simplicity itself. These machines would outsell their British counterparts but the profit margin on them would not be enormous.

With a heavy heart, he took the decision that saddens him to this day but was probably the founding of his fortune. When he returned to the North East he walked into the Scotswood Road showroom, opened only two years before in a blaze of glory, and issued his ultimatum: 'I love you dearly, George, but you see these rows of motor cycles? I'm coming through here next Friday and I want them gone ... every one of them'. The astonished Manager asked, 'How am I going to do that?' Tom Cowie's answer was abrupt: 'Burn them if you like; auction the lot. Any price will be a good price. I'm sorry, George, but we have no choice'. The George in question was George Crawford, the 'king-pin' of the north-east motor-cycle industry. He carried out his boss's orders to the letter but it broke his heart; he was never the same again.

In one fell swoop, Tom Cowie had liquidated his stock and taken the greatest gamble of his life – just in time. The 1962 accounts showed a profit of just £55,000—but at least he made a profit! Many of his competitors, clinging too long to a sinking ship, simply faded away. 'Cars were our future, if the dealerships would allow, and in 1963 Broadwood Finance (named after my home,) Broadwood Hall, was founded to meet the mushrooming demand for more extensive credit. It was a new, more sophisticated but equally sensible and conservative hire-purchase system than its simpler predecessors. This wasn't an especially happy period for Cowie's, but it was a situation we had to face head on. We survived, while many didn't, ham-strung by a combination of outdated management techniques and refusal to face the facts'.

In essence, it didn't really matter how good Cowie's were as retail dealers: without the main franchises it was impossible to progress beyond a certain point. The firm had a vast investment in commercial property but the motor-cycle market was visibly shrinking. In Newcastle, Cowie's were the poor relations to Eric Buist. George and Jobling, with its massive Northumberland territory, was in Forth Street, a mere 200 yards from Cowies' Scotswood Road showroom. Eventually, they would go into receivership and Cowie would buy them, along with their dealership, but for the moment they represented competition Tom Cowie could well have done without.

Cowies' sale of Austin cars was slowly consolidating. Newcastle, Stockton, Durham and Edinburgh saw Cowie's selling Morris vehicles (all retail dealerships and therefore second division), but at least car sales were up and running. Pre-tax profits—which, in 1961, had stood at £85,000—had, by 1965, reached £234,197. But Tom Cowie was disappointed when 1964 ushered in a new Labour government after what the media disparagingly called 'thirteen years of Tory misrule'. Out went Sir Alec Douglas-Home and his 'matchstick economics'; in came Harold Wilson and the 'white heat of technology'.

'I had long nailed my political colours to the mast. My father had embraced Conservative ideals; I had done likewise but, as a businessman, one must make the best of whatever ensues. However, I can say without reservation I was truly appalled at the prevailing attitudes which emanated from the Labour think-tanks, and the whole machinery of government, which seemed to be deliberately obstructive. At times it felt positively malicious; we felt we were fighting not only foreign competition but our own Government'. Taxes soared sky-high and dividends were hit with what he considered vindictive force. The business world was faced, as far as he could see, with people in power who seemed to possess no idea of how to run business or co-operate with industry. The accepted Socialist political, ideological line was all that mattered: If you were singing from a different ideological hymn-sheet, hard luck! This feeling that the administration was deliberately out to maul, induced in me a total alienation from what I felt was an intrusion into my business affairs.

'The motor trade revolves around the hire-purchase system. In an expanding market, where a wide variety of customers exist with a myriad of other financial commitments and priorities, the flexibility it brings, the opportunities it affords for those with less money to lay out in one go, are critical'. Now, he felt that he was facing a Government that kept moving the goalposts, challenging the rules on deposits and repayment time-scales.

'The restrictions imposed varied from month to month. Our fledgling Broadwood Finance coped with all of this, but it was an unwanted, uncalled-for sort of interference which saps morale and drains the enthusiasm of all but the most determined. I have never quite grasped the rationale behind overtly penal rates of taxation. The way I see it, the more you squeeze, the less you actually harvest. If the Government squeezes till the financial pips squeak, businesses that can't successfully ride the storm fold, or look for loopholes. People don't mind paying taxes if they feel they are equitable; if they feel they're being taken for a ride, they rebel in one way or another'.

Struggling with what he saw as a pointless mountain of fiscal red tape, desperate to obtain main dealerships, nevertheless Tom Cowie could watch his profits steadily rising. As other businesses faded, his was forging ahead because of his attention to his customers and the fact that the profit from hire purchase was going into his pocket and not to a third party.

SIR TOM COWIE

Chapter Twelve

Going Public

Tom Cowie's visit to the nine-million-pound Honda factory in Japan had depressed him. The vast research-and-development programmes and a production line producing 3,400 motor cycles a day were impressive, but also spelled out doom for British manufacturers. The trip confirmed his feeling that it was time to say goodbye to the motor-cycle business: Japanese bikes would take over the market and the profit margin on them was low. In addition, as more and more dealers were appointed, increased competition was further eroding profit. Tom drove a Honda car on the test-track and was impressed with its performance. He knew, now, that the future of his business must lie in four-wheel vehicles but, as always, he was hamstrung by his lack of main dealerships. He had Howey's on Sunderland's sea front, bought in 1962, which was a retail dealership for Austin, and other dealerships in Sunderland would follow, but a main dealership continued to elude him. He was selling Morris cars in Newcastle, Durham, Stockton and Edinburgh: indeed, his showroom in Lothian Road would become one of the biggest in the Scottish capital. BMC dominated car sales in Britain and the public were eager for their Morris and Austin cars. Tom reasoned that, if he accumulated enough BMC retail franchises, they would eventually reward him with a main dealership, but he hoped in vain. And as well as their refusal to give him main dealerships there were other matters to concern him.

'Much has been said and written by others on the wildcat strikes at Ford and British Leyland in the 1960s and 1970s, and their effect on the supply of cars to retailers. Indeed, the uncertainty of delivery played havoc with sales – planning, projections, decision-making felt like a lottery at times. Apathy on the assembly line; poor workmanship and an inferior product; increasing stridency among trade union leaders; the knock-on effect on demand, both domestic and international; the progressively shorter supply of finished vehicles—all meant trouble at a time when business should have been booming'.

For Cowie's, as relatively new car dealers, it meant that they had to do extremely good deals on the few vehicles they managed to obtain. Almost inevitably, it put the price up for the consumer and for the retailer, and cash-flow headaches multiplied. Tom Cowie looked around the car industry and saw weak, vacillating management which, in far too many cases, could not stand up to the unions. A depressing sense of everything going downhill fast prevailed. 'In Britain, motor cycles went rapidly from world leaders to also-rans, in exports and at home. Crass stupidity on the part of trade unions and management seemed likely to do the same for cars in due course. Nowadays, alas, with the sale of Rover to BMW, only small specialist concerns such as Morgan's remain in British hands, but then we had a chance to learn from what was happening to the likes of Triumph and BSA. Sadly, the lesson was left unlearned'.

Main dealerships were the key, but all he could do at this stage was to pick up retail dealerships to boost volume of sales. Many of the old family businesses were running out of steam in terms of ideas, motivation and finance. The motor business had always been competitive and, by the 1960s, a second generation of family directors was not so hungry for success. Profit margins were always small, 2–3 per cent at most, and many companies faced going to the wall. Cowies' grip on the hire-purchase market, via Broadwood Finance, improved their margins at a critical time. The New Year period and July are notoriously poor times in terms of sales. Cowies' ability to secure a fairly unwavering level of profits, via the hire-purchase trade, throughout the financial year was to reap even bigger profits in the later years when the era of contract hire was ushered in.

As the 1960s progressed, Cowie's were contemplating a momentous decision—to float the company on the Stock Exchange. To get those coveted main dealerships it had to gain funds for further expansion by the process of 'going public'. Tom was to hold a substantial share of the total issue. 'It wasn't a "megalomaniac" urge to control for control's sake; I sincerely believe that the best managers of any financial concern are those with a direct, fundamental stake in its success'.

The next stage was to find a financier sympathetic to Cowie's case, and knowledgeable as to the company's needs. Tom Cowie was not enamoured of the City, an institution he regarded as redolent of snobbery. To him, his company was the pride of his life but, to the City of London, Cowie's was small fry—a northern minnow among the southern pikes. As he searched for a dealer, he began to wonder if, within the Square Mile, a financier existed who was prepared to show a genuine interest in his project. 'I'd done the rounds and come up against a brick wall which, though not unexpected, only served to fire my enthusiasm and determination to succeed. The name Julian Hodge began repeatedly to reach my ears. Here, I was told, was a maverick, a brilliant mind, the Socialist errand boy turned tycoon, who was to be knighted in 1970'. If anyone could do the job, Tom reasoned, this Cardiff-based individual brought up in the South Wales valleys, the founder of the Bank of Wales, assuredly could.

'His costs were far less than those of his London brethren, his manner more relaxed, but his financial acumen left them all standing. Refreshing to talk to, and helpful at every turn, Julian was a most impressive man. He sat at his desk opposite me, pencil wedged behind one ear, and cut swathes through the financial fog with endearing candour and heart-warming ability. Here was a breath of fresh air; an ability to share my vision; a quick, efficient realisation of my plans—and at a quarter of the price'.

On 31 December 1964, a grand total of 2,624,760 Cowies' shares were ushered into the public domain. The price was 4s 3d in old money—almost 22p in modern parlance. It was agreed that a fair price had been found, and the vital funds for expansion would be forthcoming. The stock-market flotation went fairly smoothly, with no real complications, but now Tom Cowie was answerable to a whole new group of people—the shareholders. Wisely, he set up trusts for all his children, by now five in number. The more he could keep the business in the family, the better he liked it.

Chapter Thirteen

The Precious '123'

Before the company was floated on the Stock Exchange, Jim Barber was appointed Deputy Chairman and long-serving members of the Management Team were made directors: George Crawford, Bob Johnson, Sheila Rawlings, George Stephinson and Edgar Turner took their place on the Board. For Sheila Rawlings, it was a dream come true: from office girl at the start of the business in 1948 she had become a £2,000-a-year director at only 33 years of age. 'Sheila was a personal friend and a bridesmaid when I married Lillas, and was without doubt dedicated to the company. At the time of her promotion I described her as "a good, energetic worker". To be honest, she worked all the hours God sent for T. Cowie Ltd; she was a dedicated, loyal, industrious person. Cowie's grew rapidly; in truth, it outgrew her and there no longer seemed an appropriate niche for her to fill. There was to come a time when I felt compelled, in the late 1970s, to retire Sheila on full pay for the rest of her life. Having to do such a thing is always traumatic, but it is essential for the future well-being of the company. The same was true of Bob Johnson, another workhorse for the company—genuine, honest and thoroughly nice. He left about the same time as Sheila and for similar reasons, having been Company Secretary for a time'.

As 1965 dawned, the new Board sat down to wrestle with their biggest problem—the lack of a main dealership. However many retail dealerships the company might own, they were still all at the mercy of main dealers, who were not likely to pass on new vehicles to retailers when they could so easily sell them themselves. They were making profits, but Tom Cowie knew that becoming a main dealer would unlock new levels of profitability. He was hungry for progress, and having to be dependent on a main dealer was irksome.

Salvation came in the shape of a colourful character named Louis Playfoot. He had a Vauxhall main dealership in Redcar, Cleveland, and ill-health meant that he was willing to sell up. Tom Cowie was delighted to announce the Playfoot purchase in his Chairman's Review of 1965: 'This is our first venture into motor-car distribution', he wrote; 'I feel certain we must expand further in this field'. Tom paid £80,000 for Playfoots (including the premises, leases and stocks,) and Louis Playfoot remained as General Manager for a time. Two further Sunderland retail dealerships were the next acquisitions—Roland Monkhouse Ltd, with its Austin dealerships at Holmeside and Ryhope Road, and Theatre Garage Motors Ltd in Low Row.

Expansion was not easy in Britain in the mid-1960s. High bank rates, a credit squeeze, hire-purchase restrictions, abolition of resale price maintenance, increased petrol duty and income tax, rising overheads and labour costs, selective employment tax, and a car supply dependent on a strike-hit motor industry—these were just some of the obstacles to be overcome. 'We were able to offset some of these disadvantages by good management and hard work', Tom Cowie wrote in that same review of the year. He might also have mentioned aggressive advertising and promotional campaigns. A salesman to his finger tips, he was usually one step ahead of the competition; this made him money rather than friends in the industry.

In June of 1966, he went into print in the *Newcastle Journal* to criticise the government: 'Demand for cars will keep on rising. The future could be wonderful but Government measures are holding us back'. Not even the Government could stifle his wish to expand, however. Despite the economic problems that beset him he commissioned a new showroom in Sunderland. In true Cowie style it was a massive 32,000 feet square, and complete with a host of facilities.

'Trimdon Street was the epitome of the modern integrated service and fault-diagnosis unit—the first of its kind outside London and generally hailed as a technological breakthrough—our own little bit of "white heat". With its twin service dock, replete with steel section construction and cantilever supports, and operated by Castrol engineers, we were justifiably proud of it. One hundred and fifty checks were carried out on vehicles, and the results reported to the customer. Ironically, Trimdon Street also provided testimony to the unmitigated trial and nuisance that public officials can be, especially where compulsory purchase is involved. An extensive road-widening scheme was later devised, which would have caused problems for us if a compromise hadn't been found. The "Queen's Representative", as the pompous little official we dealt with considered himself, made a potential problem a positive headache! In my 1967 Chairman's Review of the year I described it as "the most difficult in all of the post-war years", and so it was'.

By now, Cowie's were regularly involved in negotiations with national suppliers of tyres, batteries and car accessories. If they intended to go big-time and seriously improve their margins, favourable deals became a necessity. 'As 1966 progressed, the interim reports on our progress were increasingly favourable, despite all the Labour Government seemed to be throwing in the way of spanners in the works. The press reported us as greeting the new financial year as "a challenge to their youthful but experienced team in a quiet but determined optimism". By balancing closures of unprofitable depots, absorbing stock and reducing overheads with a sensible but steady acquisition of dealerships, we felt we could justify the optimism and faith Julian Hodge had shown in our abilities'.

Broadwood Finance continued to go from strength to strength, and contributed to an otherwise disappointing annual profit of £82,000. Two years earlier, this gratifying success had led to the setting-up of a new Cowie company in the form of Broadwood Securities. Its *raison d'être* was the financing of credit agreements secured by first and (mainly) second mortgages. By 1968, the two Broadwood concerns were netting 10 per cent of the Cowie's Group profits. 'Arranging credit for our customers was thus a profitable enterprise; it was also one beset with Government restrictions, especially in the realm of conventional hire purchase. Thus the emphasis had shifted to second mortgages—a viable, logical development in view of the rising value of houses as personal equity. Viable, yes; logical, yes; but viewed as new fangled and frowned upon by the conservatively minded City institutions. Personal loans posed no such problems; hire purchase was absolutely acceptable for the masses; but second mortgages, now *that* was decidedly *infra dig.* "It simply wasn't done, old boy!"'.

Financial circles disapproved of second mortgages. They were regarded as 'seedy'—the refuge of usurers and a threat to the security of the principal lender. But to Tom Cowie there appeared to be more security in bricks and mortar than in a motor car that was subject to depreciation.

There were, of course, a number of legal hurdles to be negotiated concerning second mortgages. Cowie's were amassing quite an impressive portfolio regarding this form of finance, but a money-lender's licence became necessary. A certificate issued by the then Board of Trade under Section 123 of the 1967 Companies Act—the '123 Certificate'—was rarely granted and now assumed the proportions of a priceless asset.

The means of acquiring a '123 Certificate' were explored by the company accountants and lawyers. The existing certificates were held by banks. But how do you go about buying a bank—not a giant of Midland or Barclay proportions, but a modest, functioning bank? Enquiries were made, avenues explored, contacts urged to come up with something—and quick! Then fate intervened; a member of Cowies' own hire-purchase department mentioned a real possibility with the unlikely name of Red Dragon Securities, and it was up for sale. To Tom, it seemed that the Cowie luck was holding firm.

Chapter Fourteen

Red Dragon

Based above a garage in South Harrow, Red Dragon was a tiny company that operated a finance business with current and deposit accounts for their customers. Best of all, they possessed a coveted '123 Certificate', 'something which Cowie are likely to find especially valuable', the business press trumpeted. Here was a case where Tom Cowie's tenacity was to pay off with a vengeance: 'I kept trying to contact the owner. Ten times or more each day I rang, until eventually, after about a week, I spoke to him. Did he want to sell it? Deafening silence, so I repeated the question. Well, yes, he did. How much? Well, and here the pause was palpable, the whole situation was rather complicated. It transpired he had just sold it to an earlier bidder, Sidney Davison. Had he signed the papers with Davison? No he hadn't. How much had he been offered? A figure was quoted, and I agreed to double it. When could I see him? Tomorrow, came the prompt reply'.

Tom dashed to London with a confirmation of what he had offered on the phone. He knocked on the vendor's door, who appeared at an upstairs window, nervous as a kitten—and who could blame him, especially as an injunction from Sidney Davison had put a halt on the £160,000 deal? Papers were quickly lodged with solicitors, along with exhortations to sort it all out, and promises of double fees for a quick solution. Tom Cowie made contact with Sidney Davison and his financial feathers were monetarily smoothed; indeed, he remains a friend of Tom's today. A cheque was written and Red Dragon Securities came under the Cowie wing. 'It all sounds so simple and so quick, and in essence it was. I had bought a bank for relative peanuts, for I was to sell it in 1979 for over two million. The acquisition meant so much for Cowie's, that I'd have gone higher by far. Thankfully, the other players did not know that. In poker, in business, bluff undeniably plays its part'.

Cowie's gained great publicity from the purchase, for it was a remarkable step forward. Tom was anxious to incorporate the word 'bank' into the Broadwood name, for it conjures up the size and stability of a national institution. Browney Bank, a location not far from Broadwood Hall, was mooted but the Red Dragon Securities name prevailed. Suddenly, everyone seemed to be getting into the second-mortgages business, seeing it as a veritable licence to print money. It was a market that

Cowie's were to leave behind in a relatively short time, for the business was ruined by sheer avariciousness on the part of some operators. The commission being paid to agents in the process went sky-high. Cowie's had paid about £50–£100 per agreement; soon sums, of £1,000 were being bandied about and greed killed the proverbial goose.

'We ultimately sold the bank to AVCO in London, the sponsors of West Ham United Football club, but we had utilised a priceless acquisition to the full. It was the one and only "123 Certificate" I personally came across during those years. I'm sure there were others around, but it didn't lessen the sense of achievement I felt when I obtained one'.

The year 1969 also saw Cowie's linking up with a major finance house, Mercantile Credit. The company did a fair amount of hire-purchase agreements with them, but Tom had grown increasingly wary of this market—too small a deposit, too long a repayment and insufficient collateral left in the vehicle for his comfort. He put such business in the direction of Mercantile, who were later snapped up by Barclay's. 'There followed a fortuitous meeting as I was getting on a train at King's Cross. Soon, I was chatting over dinner to Victor Adey, the Chairman of Mercantile Credit, as we sped northwards, calculating the volume of this informal agreement we had. He mooted the possibility of a joint venture—a sharing of the profits, and the risks. Cowie's would do the underwriting; Mercantile Credit would provide the money at a sensible rate'.

Adey floated the idea of taking a share in the Cowie parent company—about a 45 per cent stake. The details were thrashed out by lawyers and accountants. Victor and one of his senior associates became Company Directors at Cowie's and, at first, all seemed fine. What finally did cause an upset was Victor's opposition to association with Red Dragon Securities, which was frowned on in the City. It is difficult to work out quite why there was such implacable opposition. Perhaps it was prejudice against 'the northern upstart'. More probably, it was less to do with Tom Cowie's northern origins and more to do with the fact that he was more daring in his approach than the established institutions. And, most unforgivable of all, he was succeeding in areas where he might have been expected to fail.

'Victor Adey and his company preferred the systems of unsecured loans. I found them an unsatisfactory and risky half-way house and, in 1973, there was a reasonably amicable parting of the ways. Cowie's even acquired the Kirby Garage group of Chrysler dealerships in the Liverpool area from Mercantile Credit for the nominal sum of one pound. Victor and his associate resigned from the Board at Cowie's. I bought some of the shares back from Mercantile, but the 45 per cent were mainly dispersed through about 10 different brokers and agents in London. It was crucial that no one was able to come in with a substantial batch of our shares. The link-up had been a mutually beneficial enterprise while it lasted. Some people may have viewed us askance, but none doubted our business acumen, and our underwriting was second to none in our field. The Cowie reputation went before us: we'd never had a debt problem, and that counts for a lot. Cowie's were legitimate in what we did; it was morally justifiable, but it broke the unwritten rules of City etiquette. Like Julian Hodge, we were outsiders—northern upstarts, and decidedly not above suspicion'.

The year 1969 ended with another victory—Cowies' acquisition of its first Ford main dealership, Brooks Motor Company of Newark, in a £182,000 deal completed on 1 December. It had been a good year!

SIR TOM COWIE

Chapter Fifteen

Farming Territory

Brook's was a large motor company based in Newark with a secondary line in agricultural machinery, but it was a very different proposition to anything Tom Cowie had tackled hitherto. Edgar Turner neatly summed up the difference: 'You can only sell a combine harvester at the beginning of harvest. And if you take one in part exchange you have it in stock until the next year's harvest'. Initially, Cowie's intended to carry on the sale of agricultural machines (even to expand the business), but it soon became apparent that this was not commercially viable. A decision was made to sell-off that side of the business—but not before they had enjoyed some 'rural' open days, including a 'Farmers' Question Time' programme chaired by the incomparable Ted Moult, then a leading TV personality.

Despite these difficulties, Brook's was an important acquisition for Tom Cowie. 'Brook's was an entrée into that special world of Ford main dealerships. Ford have a ruling that one cannot control a dealership selling other manufacturers' vehicles within 30 miles of the Ford dealership held. Also, one could not then own more than five of these Ford main dealerships, not even worldwide. Still, we deemed it worth it: by now we were rising into the big league, nudging into premier status. A long and highly successful partnership with Ford was under way'. But union with Ford did not mean neglect of other companies: in Redcar, new premises were acquired to accommodate the expanding Vauxhall dealership at Playfoot's and, in 1971, Cowie's bought Northumbria Motors in Newcastle, a Renault main dealership. This they transferred to their own magnificent Scotswood Road showrooms and held a gala opening. The ceremony was performed by Graham Hill, the motor-racing champion, while Pierre Dreyfus, the Renault boss, came specially from France to honour the occasion. He gasped at the sight of the huge area involved, exclaiming 'My God! This is bigger than our showroom in Paris!'.

Cowie's were buying up dealerships left, right and centre, but the new buzz-phrase in the industry was now 'vehicle contract hire'. As usual, Tom Cowie scented change and was ready to exploit it by forming Cowie Contract Hire. Within 12 years they would have a contract-hire fleet of 16,000 vehicles and be one of the largest in the country. Group turnover was rising dramatically: by 1972 it was £13 million, up £5 million on the year before. Now Ford began to show their appreciation. They always reserved the right to take back a main dealership if a business changed hands. When H. Young (Sunderland's main Ford dealer) was sold, Ford stepped in and offered the main dealership to Cowie's. This was flattering but it posed a huge problem: Ford would not permit a Ford main dealer to sell another manufacturer's vehicles within a 30-mile radius. If Tom Cowie accepted the Ford offer, the Renault dealership in Newcastle would have to go. He still remembers the heart-searching, the feeling that he must take one step back to take a bigger step forward.

'Here was yet another family company; the owner died, the son took over, but the economic writing was already on the wall and the company was sold. However, while Young's were entitled to sell shares, they could not sell the Ford dealership; the American car giant gets very antagonistic towards those who try. We had no trouble selling Ford cars. Ford had ample evidence of what we had achieved at Newark. A phone call from Bill Batty, (later Sir William,) at Ford convinced me that I should get on a train to London as quickly as possible. In short, Cowie's were offered the main dealership for our own home town at last. Ford wanted the best and we had proved that we were worthy. Ford's prime motivation is market share, even more than volume. The best staff and premises, the best dealers, are demanded and inefficiency is just not tolerated. The tactics are velvet gloved, but there's no mistaking the iron fist within. Some dealers fail to recognise where the faults lie bad operators, weak management and mediocre expectations. Ford circulate to their dealers details of average profits expected for the different sizes of dealership; you ignore this at your peril: Young's did, and Cowie's mopped up'.

Unlike earlier acquisitions, Cowie's didn't pay anything or take over the existing premises; they were simply awarded the Ford main dealership in Sunderland. However, there were a number of adjustments to be made to bring Cowie's into line with Ford's stringent rules and restrictions. First of all, it meant disposing of that prestigious Renault franchise in Newcastle, under the 30-mile ruling. There was regret, but it was deemed a necessary sacrifice; it was a step back, but only in order to take an even greater one forward. Ford did allow Cowie's adequate time to find an appropriate buyer for the Scotswood Road operation. This eventually materialised in January 1975 in the shape of the North Eastern Co-op. Changes also had to take place within Sunderland itself. At Norman Howey, the Austin and Vauxhall presence was replaced by Ford, while at Roland Monkhouse the Austin retail dealership also gave way to Ford. In addition to this, the Datsun main dealership at the Theatre Garage in Low Row was ended. This site reverted to its original petrol and used-car sales status, but did become the Cowie Group's main car and van hire depot on Wearside.

In 1972, Cowie's also became a Ford Truck Specialist Dealer, purchasing both a factory and two acres of land in North Hylton Road. The acquisition was followed up by extensive work to convert the premises for its specialised purpose, but the end product was well worth it: the Group could boast a well-equipped, spacious and modern premises, tailor-made for the sale and servicing of a range of commercial vehicles, and an important stores depot as well.

In the car industry as a whole, however, all was far from well. Dealers could never be entirely sure that delivery would be up to scratch or on time. Promises and projections varied from week to week. Prolonged strikes and ensuing shortages meant that car prices and profit margins rose, but that was no way to run a business. Problems over spare parts mounted; cars sat in showrooms awaiting them, taking up space. Cowie's took all sorts of measures in an attempt to lay hands on parts: when extensive phoning sessions failed, Cowie staff were sent down to London for two or three days, visiting all the Ford dealers to buy up what was available. It led to a lot of totally unnecessary paper-and leg work and made it almost impossible to plan ahead.

Existing customers, especially those who purchased their fleets from Cowie's, had their current cars to use and accommodation was reached with them as to delayed and staggered deliveries; however, with new clients, life was trickier. This didn't please Tom Cowie. What was really irksome was the way that overseas competitors muscled in, taking advantage of this malaise in the domestic car-manufacturing industry. European rivals had to be laughing all the way to the bank, and anyone with an eye to the future could see that this was laying down the red carpet for an even greater invasion from the Far East. In Britain, the building of a single car could involve four or five interruptions for strike action.

Vandalism in the factories assumed epidemic proportions: one of many regular rogue practices was to weld a milk bottle inside a car door; every time the customer took such a vehicle around a corner, the noise was considerable—but sometimes it took ages to track down the fault. The tricks multiplied as dealers wised up to the old ones. To Tom Cowie, burning to expand, this was anathema: 'Most depressing was the sense of malicious intent, of out-and-out troublemakers—communists, even—deliberately wrecking the economic endeavour of this country. Some strikes in the past had justification; nothing could begin to excuse such wanton behaviour as the seventies witnessed'.

Tom Cowie's view of the late 1960s and 1970s is coloured by the damage he believed was inflicted on his own business. The least interruption or delay was an outrage to a man already flushed with success and thirsting for more. But there is no doubt that industrial unrest was a feature of that time. Indeed, unrest even infiltrated government: in 1969, James Callaghan, then Home Secretary, was dropped from Harold Wilson's inner cabinet because of his support for TUC opposition to the controversial White Paper, 'In Place of Strife', proposed by Employment Secretary Barbara Castle. There was even an attempted coup by left-wingers to oust the Prime Minister.

By 1970 strikes were at their highest level since 1926, the year of the General Strike. Nearly nine million working days were lost that year, mainly in engineering, but there were also major disputes involving dockers, newspapers and local authorities. The three-day weeks of 1972 and 1973 caused by the miners' strike and disputes on the railways and in power stations were symptoms of something sadly wrong with the management of industrial relations. By 1974, galloping inflation had

Britain in its grip, owing in no small part to crippling wage demands. The year 1975 saw unemployment figures pass the million mark—a rise that the Chancellor, Denis Healey, attributed to those same wage demands. Extreme, Tom Cowie's view may have been, but he was not alone in believing that something was sadly wrong with Britain's economy.

SIR TOM COWIE

Chapter Sixteen

Consolidation

Whatever the mood in the country, the mood within T. Cowie Ltd was buoyant. Newspaper headlines told the tale: 'Further expansion by Cowie'; 'Cowie beats cars slump'; 'Cowie still prospering'. And all this in spite of the miners' strike of 1972, which knocked trade in the North East. Broadwood Finance and Red Dragon now had a portfolio of more than £6 million, but Tom still hungered for acquisitions. He kept an eye on every detail of the motor trade, looking for under-performing companies in likely areas, companies that might be ripe for takeover. Five Chrysler dealerships were acquired in

Liverpool and Lancashire, and Cowie now had another Ford main dealership—Walsh Brothers of Blackburn.

'Here was a fairly old-fashioned family business, passed down from father to son, and not terribly well run. Cowie's bought it very cheaply, turned it around in terms of profitability and made as much in that first year as we had paid for the business. We put in Bob Warneford to manage things. He enjoyed a fair degree of autonomy and had room for initiative. "We bought it right", as the saying goes, but Walsh Brothers had been in terminal decline and unable to afford or even envisage what we intended for its future. The business needed a total overhaul, including a radical and extensive inventory of existing stock. On their shelves we found, amongst other things, two very expensive brake vacuum units, mandatory to have in Switzerland but not so here. They were taking up space, but were never going to be sold'.

Cowie's had already devised a simple, yet effective, system of assessment and measure of depreciation. By costing the assets of company spare parts and how often such parts were moved, percentages could be assessed: 100 per cent was deemed to be above cost; between 10 and 99 per cent was cost; and between one and nine per cent meant that the spare parts were effectively worthless. A comprehensive clear-out at Walsh's followed, as it did in many companies that Cowie's took over. As Cowie's moved into new territory, it became necessary to dispense with anything that no longer pulled its weight. Thus 1971 witnessed the closure by Cowie's of its two branches of Alexander's at Edinburgh and Glasgow: for motor-bike sales they had justifiably been renowned throughout Scotland, but they never scaled the same heights with cars.

'We could have dispensed with all the motor-cycle activities and continued the branches as going concerns, but the premises were too small and inappropriate for the modern market. The car franchises held at Alexander's were retail—not main—dealerships, with all the disadvantages involved. Being a retail dealer was a thankless task. The Edinburgh site had been a prime one, but it was leasehold; the Glasgow one was a hotchpotch of old and antiquated buildings. The biggest wrench was making everyone redundant but, in business, if you do not react you're soon out, whether you like it or not'.

The purchase of Pallister, Yare and Cobb for £151,970 in 1972 yielded a Chrysler main dealership in Middlesbrough, serving much of Teesside. They had a penny-farthing bicycle in stock, probably from when the firm originally opened in 1900; the premises were almost as ancient, virtually falling apart. Tom was to sum it up succinctly at the next Company AGM: 'Parts and service are sound; sales are weak'. But it was also a main dealership, and so a vital part in the consolidation of Cowie's. A few good people were placed in key positions and the possibilities mounted.

By 1972, however, the Kirby Garage Group in Liverpool was losing money heavily. A new Group Accountant, Gordon Hodgson, joined Cowie's in 1973. His first task was to draw up plans for the drastic pruning of Kirby's. There were problems other than profitability, as Tom Cowie recalls: 'One trouble spot was the Kensington branch in Liverpool. They used to go past with monotonous regularity, shooting out the showroom windows with airguns. We put guard dogs on and they would pinch the dogs. Law and order had all but broken down and it was just impossible to make profits'.

Gordon Hodgson was a clever man—a chartered accountant who had been managing director of a steel fabrication company before joining Cowie's. As Tom Cowie welcomed him aboard, he saw him as someone who could refine and perfect the running of the Cowie financial machine.

Chapter Seventeen

Industrial Unrest

Gordon Hodgson was in his early forties when he joined Cowie's. He had worked happily for a family firm, a foundry at Tow Law, until the owner died and the son who took over dispensed with his services. He responded to an advert Cowie's had placed, and came over well at interview.

Tom Cowie liked the fact that Hodgson was Sunderland-born and had struggled to achieve an accountancy qualification by working unpaid until he qualified—evidence of an ambition akin to his own. He saw Hodgson as the answer to his prayers. For a long time he had wanted more stringent accountancy procedures throughout his company: 'I wanted regular breakdowns of all aspects of the business. Financial information is the compass of a business, just as in a ship. If the business meets with disaster the compass … the accountancy … is gravely at fault'.

Hodgson was engaged as an accountant and proved not only proficient but a workaholic, a man to whom his job was his life. Tom admired him—but that was not the same thing as liking him: 'He was a dour man, not particularly charismatic, but as a businessman I would rate him as five star'.

Within months, Hodgson had made himself indispensable. First, came the drastic pruning of the Kirby operation, and then he gradually streamlined accounting procedures. Tom Cowie was grateful, and the rewards came swiftly, in the form of both promotion and share options. By 1975, Cowie's annual turnover was running at more than £18 million and each year saw new acquisitions. Nevertheless, the company was flourishing against a backdrop of international crisis and national industrial strife.

There was an inevitability about the OPEC oil crisis in 1973: petrol supplies were not inexhaustible; they were relatively concentrated; and the Middle-Eastern states were naturally going to ration output to raise prices. There was concern but, all in all, the market-place took this in its stride; only the media went into overdrive. The oil crisis was a nuisance, but for Tom Cowie it did not have the devastating influence on the car industry that union strife produced. 'The British motor-cycle industry died in the sixties; its motor-car equivalent perished a decade later. In the former, the apathy and arrogance emanated from the boardroom; in the latter, a weak and rudderless management was dealt a lethal blow by subversion on the shop floor. All this was accelerated by European, then Asian, countries invading the domestic car market. They made stringent demands on their dealers. A sense of military precision prevailed and, to be fair, it worked. There was a much greater awareness of the concept of "customer satisfaction" and slack standards could not be tolerated'.

Tom believed that employees who came to work in filthy overalls would have a similar attitude to their work. He had seen manufacturers where cars weren't cleaned before going to the customers. It wasn't unknown for workers to eat their fish and chips, then lob the paper just anywhere, even when potential purchasers were being shown around. Standards in his own showrooms were high, but in the firms that he bought out there was sometimes a culture of *laissez-faire*. 'It is an awful feeling to open a car door in a showroom for a potential customer and catch sight of orange peel, crisp packets or chip paper inside. Dirty windows; oil on the car door handles; flat tyres, or no spare wheel in the boot … it simply had to stop, and fast. Faults lay with both workers and management. It is a tragedy that the post-war industrial workforce became increasingly and alarmingly confrontational. I recall being in a group of about 10 people shown around the Chrysler factory at Linwood. Our Glasgow hosts gave us a slap-up champagne lunch, but when we toured the factory floor you could have cut the atmosphere with a knife. Disgust, hate and envy were manifest in every sullen stare. With that hostility, it was no wonder their track records on industrial relations and product quality were so dire …

the old Hillman Imp produced there was rubbish on four wheels'.

The attitude of the workforce sprang from a sense of injustice—a feeling that, if this was all life had to offer, then why bother? It didn't help that the designers and directors seemed devoid of any flair or imagination. They were a sorry contrast to the Japanese methods exemplified by such as Nissan. Tom Cowie believed that the moment you walked through the door of a business you knew what was missing. He could detect apathy in a workforce and he tried hard to motivate his own. Forty years on, a former employee of Broadwood Finance remembers her first day at work: 'This handsome, bronzed man came in and walked up to my desk. "You're a new face", he said and sat down opposite me. "I'm Tom Cowie. Tell me about yourself"'. From that moment on, she felt that she was a vital part of the whole operation.

While Britain suffered under the miners' strike and three-day weeks were on the horizon, Cowie's was experiencing a healthy balance sheet. There was undoubtedly a depression in the North East, as the traditional heavy industries lumbered into terminal decline, but the Group was going from strength to strength.

Chapter Eighteen

Breakup

In 1972, Tom and Lillas Cowie separated. Perhaps the years of unremitting business activity had taken their toll; perhaps, like many marriages celebrated in wartime or the post-war period, it had simply reached its natural end. What remained was a mutual determination that their children should not suffer from the split. Andrew, their eldest child, was at Cambridge, studying for an MA in Land Economy. A Cambridge Squash Blue and a county player of note, he was in the Ten Nations' Top Forty. Although suffering a ruptured spleen at rugby, he was an all-round sportsman who delighted his father with his sporting and academic achievements.

Elizabeth had completed her studies at Durham High School and was now at a finishing school in Switzerland. Susan was in her first year at Leeds University and Sarah and Emma were still at Durham High School. Each day, in the aftermath of the separation, their father drove to Lanchester and collected them for the journey to school. Once they had been safely delivered, he headed for Sunderland to immerse himself in work and forget personal problems.

Three years later, Tom married Diana Evans, acquiring two stepchildren (Steven and Kate), in the process. His marriage to Diana would produce three daughters: Alex, born in 1975; Charlotte born in 1978; and Victoria, who was born in 1982. For a while, Tom and Diana lived in Cleadon, first in Mayfield Drive and then in Huntingdon House; however, after Lillas' departure to a new home in 1976, he returned to Broadwood Hall.

Settled in a new marriage, his life was becoming somewhat less frenetic. No need now to chase up every deal personally or oversee every decision himself. Gordon Hodgson was proving an able lieutenant, able to make cold, incisive judgements. This was just what Tom Cowie needed and wanted, for it relieved his own load. 'Any organisation can fall victim to what I call "BFS", the "Busy Fools Syndrome", where you end up dashing hither and yon to ever-declining effect as human resources are over-stretched. At some stage you have to be able to say, "This just isn't working, it's no longer financially viable or worthwhile" and tackle something easier in terms of profit-margin returns. And to do that, you need time to think'. As Tom enjoyed his mounting success and his extended family, he saw Hodgson as an answer to his prayers and he still acknowledges that. 'Gordon Hodgson was, and is, an extremely earnest and serious-minded individual, impressively able and a tireless workaholic. I recognised that here was someone thoughtful and intelligent, with a good brain, ideally suited to the Cowie's way of operating'. Eminently ambitious, Hodgson slotted in at Cowie's and his rise was rapid—Chief Accountant, Board Director, Finance Director, Deputy Chairman, ultimately Chief Executive.

Now all the disparate parts of the Cowie empire were renamed: the Kirby Group became Cowie-Kirby; Brooks Motor Co. became Cowie's of Newark; Pallister, Yare and Cobb became Cowie's of Middlesbrough, and so on. Cowie's had emerged as a national force almost by stealth, acquiring long-established companies nationwide, and operating them under their familiar names. By 1975, Cowie's annual turnover was running at more than £18 million.

Tom Cowie went here, there and everywhere, checking on the Group's operations, but he made sure he had regular breaks. He had done this from the very beginning, seeing time off as a necessary opportunity to recharge his batteries: 'I am sufficiently aware of my own personality flaws to know that, if I hadn't taken time off occasionally, I would have driven everyone else—friends, family and colleagues included—absolutely mad. I could always see things more clearly when I got away. It gave me a chance to pick up on what other people were thinking and doing. You must keep yourself fit, physically and mentally. I always realised that, but it assumed critical proportions as the rampant corporate professionalism of the seventies built up'.

By the middle seventies, Tom Cowie could have been forgiven for a smug satisfaction at what had been achieved. His family were coming to terms with his breakup with Lillas and his business was forging ahead. He had Gordon Hodgson to rely on and another able lieutenant in his son Andrew, who had joined him at Cowie's. The difficult days of erratic cash flow and shortage of merchandise seemed a lifetime away.

Chapter Nineteen

Acquisition

Amid all the success there were setbacks, however. The problems in Liverpool with the Kirby Group seemed never-ending as social tensions continued within the city. Then, in March 1975, the group paid £148,000 for a Mercedes, Volkswagen and Audi/NSU dealership in Spon End, Coventry and changed its name to Cowie's of Coventry. Today, Tom Cowie remembers Spon End as 'a painful experience'. It had seemed a good idea to acquire a prestigious Mercedes dealership but, from the outset, there were snags. 'Spon End was a perfect illustration of the fact that it matters not if your premises and location are prime if the calibre and motivation of the staff are below par. Trying to acquire the right staff took more time than we could allow. Good mechanics could pick and choose where to work. There existed a sort of "Midlands disease"—a malaise, a 'couldn't-care-less' attitude about being fired. Company loyalty is a crucial factor; it is a trait less easily engendered inside a large, impersonal organisation than in a small, individual company. In the North East, Cowie's were well known and respected, and success had promoted further success. I will say without fear of contradiction that, in my estimation, the North East has the best workforce around. Memories of hard times past are never far away, and a sense of commitment is evident'. The Spon End experience taught him that expansion was not as easy as he had once believed.

The following year saw a luckier purchase: Cowie's acquired Salmon & Jones of Stoke, a Ford dealership and truck specialist with a net asset value of £218,000. 'Like many before it, the outlet had not been run to best advantage, and Ford asked if we were interested. It became ours for an overall outlay of £120,000 cash. It was never seen as a long-term investment, being sold off within a few years. Ford came to us offering the deal; Cowie's didn't need to chase it. Once you've made your reputation with the Ford Motor Company, you are a "preferred candidate" when any dealerships become available. Any vendors who hold a Ford franchise must inform them when a sale is on. If the price is deemed too high, trading excessively on goodwill, Ford may consider a good return by any potential buyer on their investment less than likely. It follows that Ford would also lose out; hence, the interference and undeniably dictatorial tactics.

Margins are all in the motor trade, and Ford are no exception'.

But Ford could be greedy. If a dealership had become very successful and perhaps too big in their eyes, it was not uncommon for the territory involved to be split and another rival Ford dealer put in. The original dealer might rage, but Ford's word was law. They received figures from dealers and in turn issued details of how firms should be performing within certain maximum and minimum estimates. Like so many businesses that Cowie's had acquired, Salmon & Jones was a typical family concern started in the 1920s. The family had held on to the franchise into the next generation, but that initial drive and vision had weakened and Ford had to act.

By now, Cowie profits were soaring, and the contract-hire and self-drive sections were also doing well. Cowie Contract Hire was still a relatively small fish in swirling waters but, as Silver Jubilee year approached, Tom Cowie was celebrating a more-than-satisfactory growth rate and the market was beginning to sit up and take notice. With lease hire or contract hire, a leasing company undertakes total responsibility for the vehicle. Over a period of about three years, during which the customer never actually owned the vehicle but merely paid a monthly rental, Cowie's was responsible for all aspects of repair, servicing, tyre replacement, road-fund licence, insurance, and so forth. For the customer there was a total fixed cost, and, for a company's finance director hiring a large fleet, the worry was removed. For the lease-hire company there was the comfort of fixed, known income levels throughout the period, after which the vehicle was reclaimed and sold on the second-hand market. The process was simple, and popular.

Gradually Cowie's would acquire some very large blue-chip customers, such as IBM with their fleet of 3,000 cars and Marks and Spencer with about 700. Many contract, hire companies were to enter the business, and several got their fingers well and truly burnt. Even the Royal Bank of Scotland, with its 4–5,000 vehicles administered by Royscot Finance, was not immune. As the eighties progressed, Cowie's would buy up over 25 lease-hire companies. It is impossible to say precisely why Tom Cowie succeeded where others failed. By now he had developed an insatiable appetite for expansion and was constantly on the lookout for something to buy. But the old principle of customer satisfaction, learned at his father's knee, was also helpful. Cowie's were always ready to tailor a deal to the client's satisfaction or to make their price more competitive. Above all, there was no inclination to lie down once a plateau was reached; the word 'plateau' was not in Tom Cowie's vocabulary.

The acquisition of main dealerships and retail outlets continued throughout the 1970s. The finance division was healthy and Group profits in 1976 were yet another record—up 27 per cent to almost a million pounds.

The following year, Edgar Turner replaced Jim Barber as Deputy Chairman. Jim Barber had played a key role in transforming the Group from a small, local, motor-cycle business into the multi-faceted national company it had become, and Tom Cowie was sorry to see him go. However, having an old and trusted friend as his deputy made the transition easy, and the spiral of success continued.

By 1978, profits were almost two million and turnover in excess of fifty million pounds. Even the City, for so long sceptical about Cowies' endurance factor, was forced to take the group seriously. In that year, Cowie's finally terminated its motor-cycle dealing, although the Chairman's report promised that 'this area of our business will be kept under constant review'. Two years later, he would donate four vintage motor cycles and £15,000 to the Beamish Museum in County Durham. Tom Cowie has never wanted to live in the past, but he does take pleasure in preserving history.

SIR TOM COWIE

Chapter Twenty

More Industrial Unrest

The advent of a Conservative government in 1970 had come as a relief to Tom Cowie, who had long been one of the party's staunch supporters. 'The business world sent up a collective prayer of thanks. It felt as though peace had been declared after a long-running war of attrition against our own Government. The sense of relief was palpable; we were convinced that never in the future would we have to face worse than the Wilson administrations of the swinging sixties, when it seemed the IMF alone was staving off British bankruptcy. We welcomed "Selsdon Man" with undisguised enthusiasm'.

The election result came as a surprise to many people, as nearly all the polls had signalled a Labour victory. Outside Number 10 Edward Heath, the new Prime Minister, promised 'strong and honest government', appointing Alec Douglas-Home Foreign Secretary, Reginald Maudling as Home Secretary and Iain Macleod as Chancellor. The Tories held 330 seats in the new parliament, Labour 287, Liberals 6 and Others 7. The electorate's concern at industrial strife had proved more influential than Labour's portrayal of the Tories as 'Yesterday's Men'.

Heath's promise of strong government appeared to be fulfilled when a national dock strike, which began a month after the election and was expected to last for a long time, was settled within two weeks. In December, the House voted in favour of an Industrial Relations Court, with provisions to fine unions if disputes were not settled without striking. Similar legislation had been abandoned by the Labour government a year before, but Heath declared that the country was sick of wildcat strikes. Tom Cowie was delighted.

'I date my active participation in local Conservative politics from this time. I would eventually become Chairman of the Sunderland Tory Party in 1979 as the fight back really began, a reaction to the left-wing interventionalist management—or mis-management—of the Labour Party. True, the sheer limitations of practical, pragmatic government led to a softening of the original, radical agenda thrashed out at the Selsdon Hotel, but the U-turns and subsequent support of lame ducks merely reflected the more acceptable face of capitalism when humanity and economic common sense coincided'.

However, if Tom approved of the Government, he was not too keen on its leader. 'I was not, and will never be, a fan of Edward Heath. He struck me as a very ordinary individual, devoid of any natural spark of leadership, and I regarded his petulant antics over the European Union (EU) and Margaret Thatcher a decade later as those of a spoilt little boy. But there was without doubt a sense of anticipation flowing through Cowie's as we contemplated what the future might bring if our own well-laid plans came to fruition'. His relief was comparatively short-lived: in February 1971, Rolls Royce, Britain's flagship car manufacturer, went bankrupt. The era of 'Red Robbo' and near-anarchy in the car-manufacturing sector was looming. In spite of Cowies' increasing prosperity, Tom had a sense of foreboding as the election of 1974 showed how rocky Edward Heath's hold on government had been. Harold Wilson returned to Downing Street, but unrest in the motor industry continued.

In 1968 the British Motor Corporation and Leyland Motors had amalgamated to form British Leyland. Almost from the outset, the new company was beset by problems. The Ryder Report of 1975 was a devastating indictment of management at the only major British-owned motor manufacturer. On Ryder's recommendation, £1,400 million of government money was pumped in but, by February 1977, the company was threatening to shut down the plants to put an end to strikes, and James Callaghan, then Prime Minister, was threatening to cut off government cash.

As Tom Cowie watched the United Kingdom sliding further into recession, his anger over what was happening to the British motor industry grew. In March 1977, 3,000 striking toolmakers caused 40,000 workers to be laid off, and Callaghan warned that 'foreign firms are simply waiting to pour their cars into this country'.

To Tom Cowie's relief, the Conservatives were returned to power in May 1979, under its first female Prime Minister, Margaret Hilda Thatcher; and, in January 1981, the Government gave British Leyland a further £990 million. Even that was not enough to save three British Leyland plants from closure later that year: in November, as the company's 58,000 workers struck over pay, British Leyland teamed up with Honda to build a new saloon. The foreign foot was in the door.

Throughout this sorry tale, one figure was centre stage. Derek Robinson, or 'Red Robbo', was a shop steward at the Longbridge plant in Birmingham. In one year alone, 1978–79, he was behind 523 disputes. He was eventually sacked, describing his nickname as 'a badge of honour'. Twenty years on, he would say: 'The pressures were immense but, were it not for the ideological understanding that I had, I could very well have ended up with a nervous breakdown. Strange as it may seem, coming from a Communist, I have some sympathy with the Royals in the way they're sometimes treated by the media'.

Chapter Twenty One

National Recognition

The year 1978 saw an ill-fated attempt by Cowie's to buy the Birmingham-based Colmore Investments, with its Fiat and BL dealerships. Colmore's embraced a multiplicity of small dealerships in which Cowie' had built up a 29.9 per cent shareholding stake. Under Stock Exchange rules, 30 per cent was the maximum stake anyone could acquire covertly; once that level was reached, a potential purchaser would be obliged to put in a take-over offer, which might or might not be viewed as hostile.

Colmore was hostile to any outside bid, but the effrontery of an offer from what he saw as a 'northern upstart' was a particular blow to the Chairman's pride. He contested the bid in any way he could, and effectively squashed any chance Cowie's might have had: it was a small business, but with unexploited potential and no rival bid in evidence. Later, Tom Cowie wrote: 'I was abroad on holiday during part of the negotiations, but that made no difference. We simply didn't win the day because the Chairman had drummed up sufficient shareholder support to thwart any chances to infiltrate. Shareholder hostility does sometimes manage to stop a hostile bid in its tracks. It is undoubtedly easier if you are trying to influence large institutions with substantial stakeholdings such as pension funds: theirs is purely a financial profit-making involvement, devoid of sentiment or company loyalty. No two bids are ever the same, and personalities can and do play their part. Suffice to say, there were no real regrets or losses of sleep over Colmore's: I never like to lose, but it did not spoil my plans; in some respects, it provided valuable lessons for forthcoming battles'.

Tom Cowie's objective now was to gain a foothold in London. In 1979 he saw his opportunity. George Ewer Ltd was a garage and motor-coach group based in Stamford Hill in north London—a second-generation family concern with interests spread throughout London and eastern England. Ewers' coach division, Grey-Green Coaches, was a substantial operation with a fleet of 130 coaches and a good reputation. Ewer's was bitterly opposed to a Cowie take-over; Cowie's built up a stake of 29.9 per cent and Ewer's countered by buying Eastern Tractors—a loss-making company with nine agricultural dealerships. Ultimately, the move did not stave off the

Cowie take-over, but it meant that what Cowie's finally bought contained what Tom still calls 'a poison pill'.

'In the negotiations we dealt directly with Henry Ewer and his deputy, who was his main accountant. The private enterprise that George Ewer had originally set up was by then a public company quoted on the Stock Exchange. As with Colmore's, we picked up 29.9 per cent of the shares, though not in so piecemeal a fashion, acquiring the bulk from another chairman, Ken Bates of Chelsea Football Club. Thus, almost in one fell swoop, Cowie's were on the verge of venturing into take-over bid territory.

To say that Henry Ewer was hostile is a dramatic understatement: it was "over my dead body" hostility in every way. We were considerably smaller than the London consortium, and the personal animosity on his part was immense, even though we lunched together on occasion to discuss the future of Ewer's. Up to the time of Colmore's, such antagonism in our dealings was rare. We had no illusions that our path would always be smooth, but the attitude we encountered saw us taken aback at first'.

Ewer business was steady, yet scarcely wildly attractive. Those personal meetings probably were deliberately acrimonious and meant to discourage. Henry Ewer obviously didn't know Tom Cowie; he proved intractable to a degree that Tom found hard to fathom at times. The purchase of Eastern Tractors was meant to be the winning stroke in this frustrating tactical duel. Ewer bought nine agricultural dealerships in eastern England, collectively known as Eastern Tractors, for the princely sum of £1.3 million. This would be the 'poison pill' unpalatable to the Cowie's Board, as well as dissipating the value of its Ewer shareholding by about 3 per cent as a consequence.

All bids must conform to the rules and regulations laid down in the so-called 'Yellow Book' appertaining to public companies. Eastern Tractors was a relatively small acquisition, and Ewer didn't need shareholder approval to act. It wasn't bought with cash but with issued shares—hence the watering-down of the Cowie holding. The battle was long and bitter, with much invective. The Ewer Chairman rejected the merest thought of a merger of Ewers' £8.8 million assets with Cowie's £5.3 million. Unluckily for Henry Ewer, his stand failed to inspire shareholder loyalty: Cowie's gradually increased their holding of Ewer ordinary shares by about 700,000, which represented a 33.964 per cent stake, and just enough Ewer shareholders accepted their bid for Cowie's to scrape over the crucial hurdle: 'I can't say we handled the negotiations as well as I would have liked, but victory was eventually ours at the substantial price of £10.7 million—an overinflated price, certainly, but in the long run to our advantage'.

Soon after the Ewer deal, the economic climate changed dramatically: interest rates shot up and oil prices went sky-high. Every motor dealer in Britain was under pressure. Cowie's did not actually show a loss in 1980–81, but it was a near thing and there were times (as he struggled to reorganise his new acquisition,) that Tom wished that he had never heard of Ewer. In order to obtain the cash necessary for buying Ewer, he had sold Red Dragon Securities—the bank he had fought for so strenuously. It brought £2.2 million from AVCO

Financial Services, but later Tom Cowie would sometimes regret the sale, feeling that it would have been a major asset to Cowie's throughout the 1980s.

Gordon Hodgson was struggling with Ewers' problems—particularly Eastern Tractors, which had been substantially insolvent when Henry Ewer bought it. It owed £2.3 million more than its worth, and it took Hodgson's undivided attention to pull the business round. The huge Vauxhall/Bedford dealership in Ipswich was losing £1,000 a day and had to be closed, as did a British Leyland dealership in Bury St Edmunds. But, in spite of such setbacks, the Ewer package eventually became profitable and Tom found the Ewer staff extremely co-operative: 'I made personal visits to meet them as much as possible, believing a personal touch would pay dividends. At one point I was picked up at the railway station by a relative of Henry Ewer and there was no ill-feeling that I could sense'.

Grey-Green Coaches came under the stewardship of Andrew Cowie, Tom's son, now working within the Cowie Group. Under his direction, the business rose steadily after initial losses and was to prove an invaluable training ground for the expertise that would eventually make Cowie's one of the biggest bus companies in Britain. The Ewer take-over was important in another respect: the attendant publicity, especially in the national press, put Cowie's firmly on the national map.

SIR TOM COWIE

Chapter Twenty Two

Sunderland AFC

Tom Cowie had been a football fan since childhood. At seven, he was accompanying his father to watch Sunderland play at Roker Park. For the boy, it was a big day out: They always went in at the Roker End, and Tom would stand on the wall behind goal, usually with a tuppenny bar of chocolate in his pocket. Even now, he can remember the players—Eddie Burbanks, Patsy Gallacher, Alex Hastings, Alex McNab, Billy Murray— the names roll off his tongue with ease, even after 70 years.

At school he had enjoyed soccer and played for his school at centre-half, although he did not regard himself as a brilliant player. In 1937, his father took him to Wembley for the Cup Final, Sunderland versus Preston North End. It was Tom's first trip to London and made memorable by the awful driving of his father's friend, Inspector Wilkinson, in whose car they made the journey. In the years before the war Tom hardly ever missed a Sunderland match, but in the immediate post-war years he was more interested in his business: Saturday was the day on which his managers reported to him on the week's business, but he went to mid-week matches whenever possible. After all, it was Sunderland playing, and that, to Tom Cowie, was everything.

Sunderland Football Club had come into being in 1879, as Sunderland District Teachers' Association Football Club, playing first on the Blue House Field in Hendon. The first years were fraught with difficulty, but the early players had the will to survive. In 1882 they moved to a ground in the Cedars, then to Groves Field, Ashbrooke. There would be two more pitch changes before they arrived at a ground in Newcastle Road, on the north side of the river, and became the first club to be elected to the Football League formed two years before by the major clubs. William McGregor, the League's founder, dubbed them 'the team of all talents' and in 1892–93, Sunderland became the first winners of the First Division.

The first full season at Newcastle Road saw the team wearing the red-and-white stripes that are now their trademark. At that time, admission cost three pence. Over the years, the Club's fortunes waxed and waned: they moved to a new ground at Roker Park in 1898, and were still there when Tom Cowie began to attend, in the late 1920s. 'Many's the time I accompanied my father into that hallowed ground and I remember with pride the glory days of 1937, when the FA Cup resided at Roker'. At the outbreak of the Second World War, Sunderland was seen as a leading team, but in the post-war years success became more elusive, in spite of vast sums of money being injected by a succession of owners. In 1970, the Club was relegated for a second time, but winning the FA Cup in 1973 sent spirits soaring. Tom Cowie joined the Board of Sunderland AFC at around that time—a move he would later describe as 'the biggest single failure of my life'. The reigning Chairman at that time was Keith Collings, whose father, Sid, had been Chairman before him. Apart from a three-year spell between 1968 and 1971, the Collings family had chaired the Board for 20 years and it was Keith Collings who invited Tom Cowie to join the Board.

'When I was invited to become a director I considered it a great honour. As a shareholder, I felt a determination that the Club should thrive. Apart from a solitary FA Cup victory in 1973, the Roker crowd had had little to roar about since before the war. In the 1950s, the Club had been known as the 'Bank of England' team, run by a bunch of able and ambitious businessmen such as William S. Martin, plus members of the Ditchburn and Evans families from the Sunderland area. Unfortunately, their sons, who inherited the shares and the power, were nowhere near as successful as their fathers. Sunderland FC did better than many but a long pedigree is of little value—you're only as good as your last season, your last few games even'.

'We must have a top manager!' Tom (described by the sports journalist, Bill Bradshaw, as 'Sunderland's Millionaire Director'), announced to the *Journal*. Uncertainty over the managerial job was causing damage to morale, and relegation loomed. 'I saw the need for new stands, which would mean an outlay in excess of £2 million, but before that a top side was needed and a top manager to guide and mould them into a team that fans would be prepared to pay to see—week in, week out. Brian Clough was the man the fans wanted. Bobby Robson and Lawrie McMenemy were also in the frame, but none were available or willing. As directors, we were responsible for all aspects of the Club, employing the manager, ground-staff, 'physios' and so forth, plus making sure the team and fabric of the Club were the best we could afford. Ticket sales, laundry, physiotherapy and treatment of injuries, salaries of all the staff and players, sponsorship, publicity and community relations—it was all down to us to organise. With my political and charitable commitments, I didn't have as much time as the other directors to devote to Sunderland FC, but I felt my usual impatience over how things were being run'.

Tom began to buy up more shares as they became available, including some from Keith Collings' brother, Derek. This made the other Board members understandably twitchy. Eventually, Tom became Chairman, but the Board remained uneasy. 'The most aggressive in attitude was a director called Barry Batey, and he and Ditchburn appeared to be forming a distinct camp. I obtained further shares, this time from the *Sunderland Echo*. I didn't have a majority—about 47–48 per cent—but the biggest single holding by far'.

When Tom Cowie became Chairman, Ken Knighton was Manager. He managed to secure promotion to the First Division, but life there was tough. Knighton had come to Roker Park as a coach in 1978 and his promotion to Manager was swift. As Sunderland struggled in its new division, he clashed with the new Chairman and, four games before the end of his second season, he was sacked, along with his assistant, Frank Clark. The jokes at the Chairman's expense flew far and wide: 'Ken Knighton has a new Japanese motor bike, a Cowie-saki'; a mythical Dutch signing was dubbed a 'Cowie Van Hire'. A caretaker Manager saw the team through the four remaining fixtures, and then Alan Durban, a Welshman, was appointed to manage the team. He built a side that, in later years, was considered to be potentially among Sunderland's best.

Alan Durban managed to lift the team to sixteenth in the First Division. Among Durban's signings was a little-known striker from St Johnstone named Ally McCoist. His record at Sunderland was not brilliant—eight goals in 56 appearances—and he was off-loaded to Rangers, where he became their greatest-ever scorer and one of football's best-known faces. Sunderland's success under Durban did not last: the beginning of 1984 brought a run of seven League games without a win and Durban was out, to be replaced by one of Sunderland's most loyal ex-players, Len 'Lenny the Lion' Ashurst. Ashurst staved off the threat of relegation in 1984; however, a year later, Sunderland were back in the Second Division once more.

Now, Tom Cowie began to search for his 'dream Manager'. 'I'd interviewed Brian Clough and found him the most arrogant man I'd ever met. The Lord alone knows how I could have worked with him. Bobby Robson was the man I tried long and hard to get, but he was out for a bigger prize—managing England. He was, and is, a very personal friend—a local lad, a walking encyclopaedia of football. His managerial pedigree speaks for itself, at home and in Europe. For him, by his own recent admission, football is a sort of drug, a compulsive joy despite all the heartaches and press ridicule'.

The obvious candidate now was Lawrie McMenemy—a big and (apparently) lovable Geordie, with personality, a beaming smile and great charisma. He was frequently on television as a commentator and the team he currently managed, Southampton, was undoubtedly successful. 'I approached Lawrie on Sunderland's behalf and, after a welter of meetings, I finally persuaded him to join, for a veritable king's ransom of a salary in those days, about £200,000 per annum. For that amount I hoped and expected he'd perform miracles at Sunderland, for we would have to sell season tickets like never before to recoup the money'.

At the signing he was treated to a real Roker welcome, and was regarded rather like a god by the fans, even though Clough would have been a more popular choice. 'I received numerous congratulatory letters, with only a few dissenting voices among them. Fans were as loud in their praise as they were later to be with their vitriol. Football, at Sunderland as elsewhere, is like a religion: it's tribal warfare on the terraces and beyond, verbal and physical in nature. Local Derbies against Newcastle or Middlesbrough were deafening, electrically charged affairs. The late, great, Bill Shankly once remarked that football was far more important than life or death. Managers and chairmen, they are either heroes or villains; there's no room for anything in between'.

It seemed that Tom Cowie had worked wonders, bringing back a 'Gateshead lad made good', to Wearside—and the glory days were on their way. The crowds flooded in; season-ticket sales soared; but it was a false dawn. Today, the McMenemy name can still sting: 'He proved an unmitigated disaster for Roker Park. As far as I'm concerned, what he didn't know about football would fill a library. The lost games began to mount up, but all the excuses in the world were given. Several of the best players were sold—for example, Barry Venison to Liverpool. Player loyalty inevitably suffered and team spirit nose-dived. Internal warfare on the Board intensified, especially with Barry Batey'.

McMenemy proceeded to bring in players who were in the twilight of their careers—players he regarded as 'safe bets'. With a few exceptions, this policy was disastrous: the first five games of the 1985–86 season were lost without a goal being scored, and further relegation loomed. For Tom Cowie it was a bitter blow: 'I began to receive bad press, sickening hate-mail, threatening and often obscene phone-calls, and my car was vandalised. It was getting ridiculous and I had a family to protect, as well as my own full-time business to run. I considered the situation at the Club as mostly my fault. I'd brought Lawrie McMenemy to Roker Park. I'd gone all out for First Division success, but relegation had been the result. The feeling that I was fighting on two fronts—the Board and the fans—drained my flagging enthusiasm still further. Things had to be sorted out.

Somehow, I had to gain overall control of the Club or get out altogether. With results going so badly, an increasingly poisonous and acrimonious atmosphere was created in the boardroom, in which no one could be expected to operate efficiently'. Cowie's reasoning was that his fellow directors were men amenable to doing a deal and cutting their losses: Ted Evans was brother to his wife Diana's ex-husband, and there were others on the board he felt he could persuade to do a deal. But his chief opponent was Batey.

'I rang him, fully prepared to sit down and discuss things with him. I laid my cards on the table in what I believed was a clear, unambiguous way. It was essentially me or him: either I'd buy him out, as well as Ditchburn, Collings and Evans, or I would sell my shares to them and depart forthwith. A price was agreed; a deal was struck—or so I thought. Batey said he'd be with me in about half an hour with all the four sets of share certificates, and I agreed to have my own solicitor there to tie up the legal details. Batey duly arrived, clutching the certificates under his arm, as I sat in my office chatting to my solicitor. The cheque was ready, a receipt on hand. The deal was the certificates and control in exchange for a sum in the region of £350,000. "Oh, by the way", Batey announced casually, "My legal charges are £3,500". I retorted in clipped tones that they weren't my concern: we'd agreed a deal on the phone ... there was the cheque and not a penny more would be forthcoming; "Take it or leave it". He left it, and departed, still clutching the certificates. I was dismayed, but not altogether surprised'.

Above: 'Power Battle', April 1997.
Below: Board of Directors 1988; (left to right) Tony Hughes, Iain Jane, Gordon Hodgson, Sir Tom, Lord Elliott of Morpeth, Neil Pykett, John Lander.

Sir Tom and Lady Cowie at Holwick and Wemmergill Moors.

Above: Sir Tom enjoying a day's shooting at Holwick and Wemmergill Moors.
Below left: Kim, Sir Tom's faithful Labrador.
Below right: Sir Tom with Lord Strathmore circa 1994.

1992 Honorary Doctorate of Business Administration (Hon. DBA) University of Sunderland.

Top left: Presentation of adapted minibus and trailer, Barbara Priestman School, October 2001.
Top right: Lady Margaret Thatcher, Sir Tom, Ian Tunnicliffe circa 1980, when Sir Tom was Chairman of Sunderland Conservatives.
Below left: Sir Tom's Knighthood, Buckingham Palace, 12 March 1992, (left to right) Sir Tom's sister Emma Barfod, Sir Tom, Lady Cowie.
Below right: Sir Tom and Prince Charles. Presentation of vehicle to Prince's Trust via Cowies, circa 1990.

Beamish Museum, May 2001, following a substantial donation by Sir Tom to Beamish.

Top left: Aboard 'Seabourn Legend', Sir Tom's 80th Birthday Cruise, 9 September 2002, Sir Tom and Sister Emma Barfod.
Top right: Sir Tom and Sir Bobby Robson, November 2003, Crook Town AFC v Newcastle United FC, Barcelona Cup.
Below: Celebrating his 80th Birthday aboard 'Seabourn Legend' with family and friends.

Sir Tom making a speech at his 80th birthday celebration.

Batey disputes Cowie's version of that final meeting but does not wish to rehash what he considers an old story. He remembers the whole episode as a painful one: 'Unlike most of the others on the Board, I had a footballing background, having played for the England youth team. I wanted to see Sunderland where it belonged, among the "greats". It still rankles that Cowie, having failed to buy my shares, made no attempt to sell his shares to me. I believe I would have served the Club well. However, it is all in the past. My life has moved on'.

Cowie rang Bob Murray, whom he had earlier helped to put on the Roker Board. The successful owner of 'Spring Ram' (a Yorkshire-based company making kitchen furniture), Bob was a local lad and a Sunderland fan through and through. Up until then a small shareholder, he was prepared to put money and full-time commitment into reviving the Club's fortunes. 'I had Cowie's to run and by now I had lost heart, not least through what I saw as Barry Batey's bull-headedness. Bob Murray had encouraged me to buy Sunderland FC shares in the first place, and I was now prepared to sell them to him at no profit. Solicitors present, we effected a deal in no time at all. I resigned from the chairmanship, and severed all connections with the Club. Further humiliation was to follow in the wake of my resignation, as Sunderland slumped to the Third Division'.

It was left to Bob Murray to deal with McMenemy, who was understandably reluctant to relinquish his lucrative position. It was only when relegation to the Third Division was inevitable that he agreed to accept a package and go. Bob Murray's wry comment was that 'two things should never have left Southampton— Lawrie McMenemy and the Titanic'. The *Official History of Sunderland AFC* records, 'When McMenemy joined the Club he promised to take us out of the Second Division. Unfortunately, no one had thought to ask in which direction he would take us'.

Although he no longer participated, Tom Cowie was, and remains, keen to see Sunderland do well. The building of the magnificent Stadium of Light in 1997 filled him with pride. He maintains a box at the Stadium and, on his first visit, was accompanied by a party of Chinese businessmen. As they marvelled at the size and scope of the vast arena he felt a glow of satisfaction. It was, indeed, a mighty stadium and nothing less would do for 'his' City.

If Tom Cowie had been able to buy Batey's shares he would have had total control, with over 80 per cent. On his own admission, he prefers to be 'a committee of one'. Critics would be entitled to ask why he, a millionaire, let a mere £3,500 ruin an already agreed deal: some would call it the action of a spoilt child, unwilling to yield position; others would say that he stood by a principle. If he had swallowed his pride and obtained absolute power, would he have taken the Club to greater glory? We will never know.

Chapter Twenty Three

Lease Hire

The purchase of Ewer's had been a watershed for the Cowie group: 'In terms of logistical and geographical presence, financial growth and rapidly enhanced reputation, its importance cannot be overestimated. We became a force to be reckoned with, an increasingly major player in the lease-hire stakes'. Cowie's had always followed the principle of keeping borrowing to an acceptable level. But big companies can borrow from the big banks at very competitive rates, and deals such as Ewers' meant that Cowie's were now in a position to consider borrowing in terms of millions.

Nor was Tom Cowie too perturbed by the loss of Red Dragon Securities (RDS), sold to AVCO to further his purchase of Ewer's. 'Our ownership of RDS was considered a stumbling-block in the Ewer negotiations. Tighter banking rules, to prevent a disastrous repetition of the 1973–74 secondary banking crisis, would have made a transfer of ownership increasingly difficult. It was also thought that Red Dragon Securities would be better placed for expansion as part of a large financial group with access to resources on a scale that Cowie's couldn't then provide. Added to that, our financial position was more flexible. We were given assurance that the 20 or so staff would have their interests safeguarded, along with those of the bank's depositors and customers. Red Dragon Securities even continued for a time to operate from Millfield House in Sunderland until other premises were acquired'.

The second-mortgages business had done wonderfully well for Cowie's, but the ensuing bandwagon, demanding colossal commission fees, ruined things: several companies eventually went bust because of the crazy levels of trading. As soon as there was a drop in the housing market, such companies had no real collateral. There were thus no real heartaches at Cowie's over selling; it was the right thing to do at the time.

As the eighties dawned, Cowie's were one of the few firms in the motor dealership world in profit, even if, initially, it was a close-run thing. Ewer's was a financial drain: Grey-Green lost over £250,000 in 1981, mainly on its Express Coach Services from East Anglia. Things were so bad that it was forced to withdraw from the British Coachways consortium, and problems were compounded by an almost-total collapse in the used-coaches market.

De-regulation, ushered in by the Tories in 1987, was the undoubted saviour of the coach business in general, and of Grey-Green in particular. Wonderful opportunities for expansion then arose and, by acquiring Grey-Green, Cowie's were launched into the 'big time' alongside companies such as Stagecoach, First Bus and Go-Ahead.

From the early eighties onwards, Cowie's were prepared to invest money in improving vehicles and structuring the service to be provided.

But in those early days after the Ewer purchase, the situation was not so rosy. 'We had inherited a company which owed £2.3 million more than it was worth. Gordon Hodgson had a considerable headache to deal with—a seeming 'no-hoper' of a group that suffered from poor management, but which possessed sites of increasing value. It needed all of Gordon's acumen and drive to make it pay'.

Visits to Nigeria and the Gambia were made to regain some of the money owed. Nigeria proved to be an amazing place, where bribery and corruption were endemic: on arrival at the airport, negotiation was needed to get even the most basic of services. Threats and coercion were commonplace and it was not an experience Tom Cowie relished; nor did he enjoy other aspects of Ewer trade.

'Despite the lessons learned at Brook's, we were scarcely experts in dealing with the sale of agricultural machinery, but were prepared to learn. It is essentially seasonal low-margin stuff, with local contacts among the farming community an absolute necessity. Like farming itself, it involves long hours and excessive application, and is very cash intensive. Getting money out of farmers is an art-form on its own, despite the heady promises uttered on open days. Haverhill was a world away from Hylton Road and not exactly what I'd envisaged back in 1949, but we made it pay eventually'.

In the wake of the sale of Red Dragon Securities, the Cowie Group decided to create a new venture company. A joint partnership was duly launched between Cowie Contract Hire, Broadwood Finance and the Midland Bank's finance arm, Forward Trust. Midland Bank were extremely appreciative of the high-profit potential of contract hire and were prepared to give Cowie's its backing: they provided the money; Cowie's provided the expertise.

A Board was set up with two or three directors from each partner, getting together for regular quarterly meetings. 'All went well until Midland bought a dreadful bank in the USA, Crocker, and came a right cropper … Our initial contact with the Midland Bank when the venture was set up was excellent, but their original representative was sent troubleshooting to the United States and his replacement left a lot to be desired, as far as we were concerned. We subsequently bought out Forward Trust in a very good deal. With both Forward Trust and Mercantile Credit, the trouble came when our banking partners altered their policy. When we resisted this change they wanted out. Considering how Cowie's blossomed, both may have regretted their actions'.

In 1982, Cowie's had over 3,500 vehicles on lease hire and was ready to lift off with the eighties boom in lease and contract hire.

SIR TOM COWIE

Chapter Twenty Four

Not How Many but How Much

Now the Cowie Group looked for fresh fields to conquer. They found one in the shape of Interleasing—part of the huge Hanger Investments, which operated four Ford dealerships (two in Birmingham, one in Nottingham, one in Leicester) and also a Vauxhall dealership. Gentle probing indicated that Ford would look favourably on a Cowie bid for Hanger. This was an important factor, for if Ford withdrew the franchise from Hanger when it was sold, the buyer would purchase a mere shell.

The Ewer take-over had raised Cowie's national standing and Tom Cowie felt able to step-up pressure in their bid to acquire the Midlands-based consortium. 'For me, it felt almost like a personal crusade as I'd ambitions in that direction since about 1972, when I had first met the Hanger directors. I'd lunched at the Leofric in Coventry with the Adams brothers a number of times to remind them of our continued interest, and various discreet but probing phone calls had ensured that they knew we were serious. Now, while I can in no way compare Peter and Geoffrey Adams with Henry Ewer in terms of the friendliness of their reception ... they both exuded charm aplenty ... I was but small fry in their eyes. They swam in deeper waters, and while my ambitions were received with polite bonhomie, that "Tom Who?" tag seemed to be lit by neon. Here was the northern tradesman approaching the "hunting, shooting and fishing" fraternity and, in my heart, I knew we would have to grow before we could walk through the front entrance'.

Hanger's was yet another family business created a generation earlier; however, as the 1970s progressed, it was losing its momentum and drive. Unlike Spon End, it represented a major step into the Midlands. The potential was enormous, especially after Interleasing was set up. Meanwhile, Cowie's were acquiring assets and status, and had the priceless 'preferred customer' position in the eyes of Ford, without which the Cowie bid would have been dead in the water. Ford franchises were economic lifeblood and Hanger held four such dealerships while their profits were declining into loss in 1982–83.

'Our five-million bid for these four dealerships, a London-based Vauxhall one and Interleasing, was put forward on 21 February 1984. Four new Cowie ordinary shares plus 346p cash were on offer for every nine Hanger shares, though alternative offer proposals were also put to the Hanger shareholders. Here was an agreed bid—a take-over recommended by Hanger Chairman Peter Adams and his brother and fellow director Geoffrey. Directors Peter Stevenson for Noble Grossart and Peter Cadbury for Morgan Grenfell were in full agreement, both deeming the bid "fair and reasonable". Thus, there was total accord, endorsed by Ford, that the activities of both motor groups were complementary and that improved overall results would be attainable through this amalgamation'. Cowie's would acquire other small, badly run lease-hire companies in following years, but Hanger's was the supreme acquisition. The Adams family took Cowie shares at 10p; by the 1990s, these shares topped £4, enabling the Adams' to capitalise on the sale of their family business.

The purchase cost Cowie's £5 million in cash and shares but it more than doubled Cowies' turnover, to over £200 million. Profits, too, were up more than 100 per cent, with Interleasing alone contributing over £1 million. Cowies' contract-hire fleet now comprised 16,000 vehicles, making it one of the largest in the country. In addition, Andrew Cowie had started a new fire, safety and security company, which was making a useful contribution to Group profits. There was only one drawback to all this burgeoning success: Ford have a ruling that no group can hold more than five main dealerships. Cowie's now had nine, so four would have to go. In fact, Tom Cowie disposed of five dealerships—

those that were faring least well—thus leaving himself free to snap up another, lucrative one should it become available. In a streamlining process, every dealership that was not thought to be a long-term prospect was sold. The result was a further doubling of profits.

By 1985, Grey-Green Coaches had become Britain's third-largest independent operator. Eastern Tractors was among Britain's largest Massey Ferguson suppliers, and the fire and safety division was prospering.

Increasingly, Tom Cowie saw leasing as a lucrative proposition. It is vital in lease hire to have a certain critical mass. Overheads remain relatively constant whatever the size of the fleet. If lease-hire rates are too low, or you have too small a fleet of vehicles, economic limbo is the result. Economies of scale really come into their own – 5,000 or 20,000 vehicles, the premises and staff needed are virtually the same. The cars are with the customers, not sitting on the forecourt. The business is not labour intensive and so profit margins can soar. There is none of the December–January and June–July doldrums of vehicle sales to hinder planning. Only sufficient size and efficiency is necessary to take advantage of the market.

The joy with Interleasing was that Cowies inherited not an ailing concern but the veritable 'jewel in the Hanger crown'. Without it, the Hanger deal would not have interested the Group. Based at Broad Street, Birmingham, its 8,500 vehicles were warmly welcomed into the Cowie fold.

Yet not every aspect of the take-over was smooth and unruffled, and it was in the lease-hire section that the problems arose. Interleasing deeply resented the Cowie bid and the intrusion it represented, and its top people left *en masse*. Alex D'Adda—a highly personable individual, ambitious and able in equal measure—had headed Interleasing. It was his 'baby': he had personally set it up and nurtured a network of good customer connections and efficient operating systems. 'The Cowie way' of doing things was not to his liking. A number of his colleagues felt similarly, and all went their separate ways. Neil Pykett, who had been with Hanger since he was 15 and who was running the Leicester franchise quite successfully, was put in as joint manager of Interleasing. His partner in charge was the accountancy-trained Tony Hughes from Cowie's in Sunderland, and they proved an extremely able partnership.

The atmosphere at Cowie's, if not its ethos, was changing. Edgar Turner summed it up: 'The change from how many to how much had arrived'. The emphasis was on accounting procedures, and these were reviewed at monthly accounts meetings. In July 1985 the Cowie Group bought the remaining 50 per cent of shares in Cowie Financial Services from Forward Trust for £1,627,000 in cash. Increased borrowing was needed to finance this, but in view of the Interleasing acquisition it made sound commercial sense. The July Interim Report talked in glowing terms of good progress on property disposals, but increased interest rates meant that Cowie's would have to slightly dampen-down forward forecasts. Turnover was approaching the £218 million mark, and the Report envisaged yet another doubling of profits—as, indeed, was to be the case.

In spite of such success, Tom Cowie was still irked by the reluctance of City commentators to accept Cowies' upward move: 'Confidence is vital in business, though one has to be realistic. City analysts, on the other hand, are a very different sort of beast—gloomy, Cassandra-like beings—who appear to love casting a pall over one's thoughts and plans. We were cautious, but they made us seem unduly headstrong. I do have some very dear friends in the City, but even they are positive masters of the art of financial nit-picking. The ongoing cynicism that often prevails has always been a spur to me, and I'm not above a bit of innocent point-scoring when the odd opportunity arises'.

Such an opportunity arose when Tom was staying at the Savoy after a Company meeting, the results of which had been wired to the City. After taking a phone call, he had just replaced the receiver when the ringing tone started. 'Normally, our man in charge of publicity, the redoubtable Corporate Communications Manager Robert Blower, handled such calls. He was otherwise occupied, so I answered it with a brief, impersonal "Cowie's PLC". Who was it but this analyst who revelled in virtually writing us off every year with his "Cowies' shares to go belly-up" routine. He gave his name, then launched blithely into his request: "You prepare a very nice pack with your figures, can I possibly have one?" "Why do you need it?" I enquired innocently; "You already know the results. You wrote about us last year. I was so very sure you knew what you were talking about." A short but significant silence was broken by a slightly edgy "Who is that?" and I duly informed him. "Oh!, Will you send me a copy?" he continued, having recovered his composure. "No, I bloody well will not!" I retorted. That story still induces a warm glow of personal satisfaction'.

The Cowie Group now decided to acquire shares in Godfrey Davis and amassed 4.9 per cent. 'It was our policy to build up stakes in companies—Ewer's, Appleyard, and the like—on the off-chance it might lead to further opportunities for mounting a bid. If it didn't materialise into anything, we sold our stake, always at a fair old profit. It was fun, even a bit commercially cheeky at times, but the publicity was priceless as well as free. The audacity had rivals guessing "What will these northern devils do next?"'.

Sadly, for Tom, the midsummer of 1987 saw Edgar Turner retire from his position as Deputy Chairman. His role was filled by the workaholic, Gordon Hodgson, whom Tom held in such high esteem. Andrew Cowie became Joint Managing Director. This would give rise to an undercurrent, a feeling of 'political manoeuvring'. Tom Cowie was getting older. The logical heir-apparent, his son, was still young, and Gordon Hodgson was getting restless. The old, easy relationships that had prevailed at Millfield House were beginning to deteriorate.

SIR TOM COWIE

Chapter Twenty Five

Synergy

In 1985, Tom Cowie's letter to his shareholders had talked in terms of 'moving to become primarily a finance rather than a motor-retailing group'. The thinking behind this strategy was simple: motor trading brought in 2.5 per cent; finance paid 15 per cent. But motor sales gave rise to financing and could not be ruled out. 'Synergy' had become Tom Cowie's favourite word.

In July 1987, Cowie's proposed buying the 'contract-hire, leasing and fleet management, car retail and certain aspects of the agricultural machinery and fuel-oil distribution business from Gerald Ronson of Heron Motors Ltd' Here was a group embracing seven main dealerships and a contract-hire company, Herondrive, with over 8,500 vehicles. It was just what Cowie's needed, and Ronson was a friend of Tom's. He would later serve a jail sentence for share manipulation in the 'Guinness Affair'.

Geographically, the Heron Group straddled the country. The proposed acquisition would eventually bring in Clark Brothers at Cawthorne Road, Peterborough; Keith & Boyle of Willesden in London and Buckingham Avenue, Slough; Heron of St Asaph in North Wales; Heron & Drakeson in Chester; plus Heron Fuels and Heron Tractors, also in the Principality.

Added to this were two very prestigious outlets— Rossleigh, and the Scottish Automobile Company, which operated out of Dunkeld Road and Gleneavon Road in Perth. Jaguar, Rolls Royce, Volvo, General Motors, Land Rover and Range Rover franchises would also be transferred. Herondrive itself would come under the Cowie Interleasing wing. The proposed price was £11.17 million, but H. R. Owen and Hollingdrake were both to be retained by the Heron Group. Any franchises that Cowie's couldn't renew after completion would be excluded from the package and adjustments made. 'Like the Hanger deal, the Heron acquisition was a friendly, civilised affair. I knew and liked Gerald Ronson, who headed the Group, and we have remained friends ever since. He hoped to concentrate more on property deals, and so—in terms of finance and commitment— Herondrive, especially, was no longer something he wished to hang on to. The terms negotiated were deemed beneficial for Heron. Herondrive, in turn, made our Group the largest UK operator in the lease-hire and fleet-management service sector, with 34,500 vehicles now for hire. This was following closely on the heels of the smaller Foley and Tameside acquisitions. Meanwhile, we'd sold our holding in Godfrey Holdings Ltd, to add to our liquid assets'.

Around the same time as the Heron deal, the Cowie Group also bought, from Mann Egerton, the two motor dealerships at Elmstead Road, Colchester and Risbygate, Bury St Edmunds. These Rover Group franchises were acquired for £2.31 million. Thus, in the course of two deals, nine prestigious dealerships (plus a presence in Scotland), were obtained. Cowie Group sales of new vehicles were set to exceed the 20,000 that had been achieved in 1986.

The lease-hire and motor-retail figures were improving, as were those of the coach and bus division (mainly because of the redirection of operations towards London bus routes). All was poised for financial and commercial take-off as de-regulation swept in. The agricultural sector remained depressed, but construction- and horticultural-equipment sales were moving in the right direction. Even the fire, safety and security division was holding its own.

Further sales of shares were made to raise capital and, as the autumn of 1987 approached, Cowie's bought Marley Vehicle Leasing for £16 million, and a further 5,000 lease hire-vehicles came under Cowie Interleasing control, boosting their national share to 42,500.

By 1987, the finance division provided 60 per cent of Cowies' trading profits, but retail outlets also prospered, as demand for new vehicles was buoyant until the

October stock-market crash of that year. The crash brought difficult times for Cowie's, as it did for others: their new share issue was undersubscribed, and £75 million was wiped off the value of existing Cowies' shares; however, it checked rather than halted progress. 'My eternal message was to maintain a careful "good housekeeping" ethic, as Cowie's did with the banks', recalled Tom. 'It was thus particularly irksome when the Canadian banks with whom we'd arranged the revolving credit deal got so twitchy. I met with one of their European reps at the Connaught as the pressures on us mounted. We were deemed not to have hedged our money rates enough: "Are you likely to ride out the squeeze?" was the ever-recurring mantra, a theme that tried my patience to the limit.

I caustically explained that all my personal wealth, family-trust funds and so forth were tied into the company. Was I likely to risk so much if I lacked confidence in the viability of its future and methods? This was met with typical banking "flannel", to which I retorted that he seemed in the grip of manic depression and ought to take a close look in the mirror. He wasn't exactly enamoured with my blunt analysis, but within a year he had been fired! By this time, despite the obvious strength of the commercial synergy argument, my enthusiasm for dealerships was waning a bit. It seemed an extremely hard way to earn those 2–3 per cent margins, and the brand name and location of the franchise became ever more important'.

The purchase of Reliance Leasing brought in a further 3,300 vehicles. Finance-division profits were up by 48 per cent on the previous year. Indeed, by the August of

1988, an 85 per cent increase could be discerned, with profits of nearly £6 million in the first half of the year alone.

The sales and acquisitions continued. The Heron & Drakeson dealership at Sealand Road, Chester was sold, while, at virtually the same time, Hughes Daf Ltd and Whitehall Lodge Finance Ltd were purchased from the Paul Sykes Group Ltd. Hughes Daf was a coach dealer and distributor, while Whitehall Lodge provided HP facilities for some of the Hughes Daf customers.

Between Grey-Green and Hughes Daf, the Cowie Group learned how to run a bus company and operate bus and coach leasing. This stood it in good stead in the wake of de-regulation in 1987. Via Hughes Daf, they were able to purchase vehicles from the Dutch manufacturers, Daf, at preferential rates, though this was not the rationale behind the deal: acquiring the leasing side, Whitehall Lodge Finance, was more important. 'I was very excited about the acquisition, a link-up which strengthened the coach sector of Cowie's, a good supply route and leasing experience. It was too good to miss, and the £3 million annual profits were also very welcome. Paul Sykes himself was a very interesting man to do business with, extremely down to earth, a natural entrepreneur. He had built up his Cleckheaton-based company, a town synonymous with the old Panther motor-cycle manufacturers, and was changing direction. Like Gerald Ronson, he saw his future in property deals. All this was extremely satisfying on a personal as well as a professional level—a real adrenaline rush, and very rewarding when you got it right. There were the occasional sleepless nights when I reflected on what was proposed and the figures involved. I certainly had them over the Hanger deal, but that's part of the overall fascination. You must be, and be seen to be, in charge, with facts and figures at your fingertips. You must be sure of yourself and your objectives, as there are so many other factors (like the fiscal and monetary whims of central government), outside your control. Rationalisation had to be part of the planning, and then a careful build-up of key customers – IBM, Northern Dairies, Marks & Spencer, etc. Once Cowie's had acquired Hanger's and could assure potential customers that firms such as Price Waterhouse believed the company to be reliable, the blue-chip fraternity took Cowies' credentials seriously'.

If anything characterised the Cowie Group advance in the 1980s, it was 'commercial synergy'. Cowie Interleasing shone, and alongside this the dealerships prospered. The two went together quite naturally—and without the franchise outlets the better deals on hire purchase and servicing would not have been as easy. Dealerships that are replacing in the region of 25,000 vehicles to update the lease-hire division every year can expect to get superior deals from the manufacturers. Cowie's, with more than 45,000 vehicles, were among the leading contract-hire companies in the world.

The mopping-up of occasional dealerships and smaller lease-hire companies continued from London to Leeds and up as far as Edinburgh, netting a further 9,000 vehicles and their related contracts. Typical was the acquisition in 1989 of freehold land to develop as a motor dealership at Wiggin Road, Birmingham, plus adjacent land for contract-hire sales and administrative offices. Here, Cowie's could develop purpose-built accommodation for their leasehire division, to replace the increasingly inadequate premises at Broad Street. So many companies had been amalgamated here, that further development of this sector demanded a centrally based, state-of-the-art headquarters to match.

'As the 1990s were ushered in, we were redeveloping the Land Rover, Range Rover and Jaguar dealerships at Perth at a cost approaching £1 million. A year later, the Midlands once more claimed our attention as Cowie's acquired and developed a vehicle-storage and refurbishment centre at Middlemore for £1.5 million. Small beer, in many ways, in the overall scheme of things—but all part of that commercial synergy vital to expansion, as we needed a large complex to repair and service all the fleet vehicles at the end of their leasing phase. As in all our other sectors, we had stringent Cowie standards to maintain, and the premises was solely concerned with the rigorous mechanical makeovers of vehicles ready for the second-hand market'.

By 1991, only 6 per cent of profits in the motor division were from the (then depressed) car market. Cowie's had secured the largest single car order ever placed with a British distributor, to supply over 90 per cent of Hertz UK's vehicle requirements. Blue-chip customers served by Cowie Interleasing topped 60,000 and Broadwood Finance was flourishing. Early in 1991, Cowie's sold their self-drive rental business in Manchester and Wolverhampton in the New Year but, as 1991 was drawing to a close, new acquisitions replaced them, such as the £32 million Royscot Contracts arm of the Royal Bank of Scotland.

As 1992 dawned and the nation was gearing up for the General Election, Cowie's, among others, were concerned as to what the future might hold. A Monopolies and Mergers Commission Report in February optimistically recommended the relaxation of certain franchise restrictions on new-car sales, though Tom Cowie considered it tinkering at the edges.

'We agreed to sell to Cedarholm & Voss PLC our freehold interest in office buildings at Kings Court in Sheffield for a cash consideration of £7.5 million. This was our sole major move into the property business, but it happened ultimately to coincide with a downturn in property sales and prices. Still, even here we made a profit, though it was an indicator that maybe we should stick to the business we knew'.

As the summer approached, the Cowie Group was poised for further expansion. Pre-tax profits for 1991 topped £18 million and net assets were set at £92.08 million. The pre-tax figures for the first half of 1992 showed a heartening 48 per cent rise. But Cowie's were now into a decade which was to witness dramatic changes, not least for Tom Cowie himself.

Chapter Twenty Six

Honours

As 1991 drew to a close, the British economy remained comparatively fragile. Faint stirrings of recovery had occurred in the spring, together with talk of 'green shoots' of recovery—but consumer confidence was low and unemployment rising. While the economy waited for Christmas cheer, however, Tom Cowie was a happy man. In 1982 he had been awarded an OBE; now, on 30 December 1991, a letter arrived at Broadwood Hall from Sir Colin Cole, KBC, KCVO, TD, FSA, the Garter Principal King of Arms. Tom Cowie was to be knighted by the Queen for public and political work.

A special *frisson* was attached to reading the envelope and letter. Her Majesty had been 'graciously pleased to intimate her attention to confer the honour', it read, and Tom was duly called into the College of Arms to sign the Roll of Knights Bachelor. It was now his right to apply for a Grant of Arms and Crest by Letters Patent under the hands and seals of the King at Arms. He would prepare and forward the necessary Petition for the Cowie signature, and Tom was invited to join the Imperial Society of Knights Bachelor.

As January 1992 drew to a close, a further letter arrived, this time from the Central Chancery of the Orders of Knighthood at St James's Palace. The Investiture would be on 12 March at Buckingham Palace. 'I was to arrive between the hours of 10.00 a.m. and 10.30 a.m. In bold type, I was informed that late arrival beyond 10.50 a.m. would result in my missing the Investiture on that date. Had any, I wondered, been so unfortunate in the past as to miss their moment? Given the gridlock which sometimes bedevils London, the possibility was a real one. I was to guard this letter with my life, it hinted, as no other card of admission would be forthcoming. Two guests were allowed, and I decided that Diana and my sister Emma were to be mine, so that no charge of paternal favouritism could be levelled in my direction. Instructions on mode of dress were precise— in my case either morning dress or a dark lounge suit. Decorations and medals were to be omitted. Members of the armed services were similarly instructed, and swords were also forbidden for the ceremony'.

There would be no photography during the proceedings, but all Investiture recipients would be sent commercially recorded videotapes of their moment of glory as part of a special 25-minute documentary 'strictly for private use only'. Awards would be presented in an envelope, together with details of the service and an order form for certificates, complete with appropriate fees. In block capitals, recipients were forbidden to open the envelope until the Investiture was over, although no mention was made of the fate of those who ignored this instruction!

Such formal events can be nerve-wracking to the participants, and Tom Cowie was no exception. 'It helped that I knew the Queen's equerry in charge that day, Sir Blair Stewart-Wilson. When you've shot game together and are thus on Christian name terms, you feel you've got an ally for the occasion. It was nice—as we were being shown where to stand, what to do and in what order—to hear the equerry, after referring to "Vice-Admiral" or "General", say "Tom, you'll stand there ...". I didn't trip over or rustle anything, sneeze, go the wrong way or out of running order—indeed, all was organised with typical British style and *élan*. I had my 30-second "chat" with Her Majesty, which began largely along the lines of "Well, Sir Tom, these circumstances are rather different from the last time we met ...". Since that was in somewhat different attire on a blustery grouse shoot in distant County Durham, that was an understatement— but such details do help steady the nerves and make the exchange of words more meaningful'.

It had been a long and eventful journey from Westbury Street to Buckingham Palace, and Tom felt justifiably proud: 'For me, for my family, it was a day to remember and treasure, including a delightful meal at the Connaught afterwards, together with Lord Elliott and his wife—moments when memories and emotions are allowed to go into glorious overdrive.

I duly applied to the Imperial Society for my Certificate of Authentication, indicating I would wish to be known forthwith as "Sir Tom Cowie OBE". My name appeared on the list of new members in *Chivalry* (the Society's newsletter), and I digested *The Story of the Knights Bachelor,* written by their Clerk to the Council, Robert M. Esden, with its history and detail of the award. Would that my parents had been alive to see it! Such happenings were beyond my imaginings as a little Sunderland lad. The vast majority of people at Cowie's were delighted on my behalf, and I made much of the fact that it was an award for the Company and all it had become. What's more, I genuinely meant it'.

Despite his achievements in the field of business, there is no doubt that this honour was secured for him by the Conservative Party, for his loyalty had never been in doubt, especially after the advent of Margaret Thatcher. 'I've made no secret of how I regarded Edward Heath, and for me it was joy unbounded when Margaret Thatcher snatched the Tory leadership out of his Europhile grasp. When she emerged as Britain's first woman Prime Minister, there was a sense that now, things would be put to rights—now, Britain might truly be great again. Thatcher was essentially an inspirational leader, a conviction politician prepared to tackle any obstacles with root-and-branch efficiency and vigour. The unions were tamed and disciplined, which had to happen. Certainly, there was a move away from "One Nation" Toryism, from the ideals embodied in the words of such as Macleod and Macmillan, but the more rigid, ideologically based agenda ushered in was both necessary and inevitable. Look at Thatcher's track record in the 1980s! Few others could have achieved it, and the running joke that she was "the best man in the Cabinet" had validity. The iron fist was rarely sheathed in the velvet glove, and those who stepped out of line were well and truly "hand-bagged". Margaret Thatcher's tragedy was that the power went to her head and she began to ignore her friends and believe in her own infallibility. Sir Geoffrey Howe was no traitor, but even he could only take so much. The craziness of the introduction of the Poll Tax at those punitive rates, especially a year early in Scotland, beggars belief—but Maggie was special, and in an era of men I consider political mediocrities (such as Clinton, Chirac and even Major), such talent, such conviction is sadly missed'. Would Tom Cowie have risen to great heights if he had entered national politics? That we will never know, for his political ambition was limited to his own backyard.

'Local politics—the only type I ever considered getting involved in—can often be even messier than national, and is certainly more vitriolic and personal. I had felt in the 1970s a need to get involved, and I joined the Sunderland branch of the Conservative Association'. Tom became a member of the Conservative Board of Finance's Sunderland committee, then its Treasurer, and a member of the Northern Board of the Conservative Executive Council. In 1979 he was to become Chairman of the Sunderland Conservative Association and in 1982 he received his OBE for political services.

'I have to admit I'm not a devotee of long committee meetings in smoke-filled rooms. It was sometimes internecine warfare. I recall my first speech, which suggested that if only they would fight the enemy the way they fought one another we'd win hands down. It provoked not a few sharp intakes of breath and metaphorical ruffling of feathers, but it was the plain, honest truth. Post-mortems over petty grievances are such a bore, but this is one of the problems when volunteers, not paid people, are involved. Energy and goodwill undoubtedly abound; the coffee-morning fund-raising circuit works wonders; and it is difficult to be rude when you need every vote you can get. I'm not a politician at heart, even though I do care deeply about the Tory cause'.

One job he did enjoy was interviewing prospective parliamentary candidates, though he was sometimes critical of applicants. 'There is a definite "type" that go in for it now—pushy, go-ahead and possessed of a considerable ego. Sad to say, many seem to be looking beyond the 5- to 10-year parliamentary stint towards lucrative directorships. It has become a job, not a mission, for too many, and the quality of the product has dropped. During my years as Constituency Chairman, I was ably and selflessly supported by my deputy, Ian Tunnicliffe. Intelligent, positive, and possessed of a considerable knowledge of what was involved, his contribution made it possible for me to do my job'. Almost 20 years on, Tom describes him as 'indispensable'.

That Sir Tom enjoyed his title is not in doubt, but he was not dazzled by it. 'It made no difference in the commercial world—it is far too hard-headed a place for that. You get better service in restaurants, or seats on planes; the kudos is there, but the rewards are purely social. In the area of fund-raising it has its advantages, but ultimately it's just a great honour'.

There were further honours in the offing. In April 1994, Tom received a letter from Colin Sinclair, the Chief Executive of Sunderland City Council, offering him the Freedom of the City—the highest honour the council could award. There were to be two other recipients—Eric Bramfitt, one-time Labour leader of the Council, and Jimmy Montgomery, the former Sunderland goalkeeper and hero of the 1973 FA Cup win. Tom Cowie was delighted at such a gesture from the City he loved; his delight was short-lived. 'The next thing I knew concerning the matter was another letter from Colin Sinclair, conveying his sincere apologies that the City Honours Sub-Committee was not going to proceed with the Freeman awards for 1994, owing to "the financial restrictions placed upon the Council". I replied on 30 April, indicating my genuine disappointment, but expressing a willingness to stand down if the other two nominees were allowed to stand'.

Meanwhile, local press coverage was gathering pace. On 27 July, the *Sunderland Echo* talked about the City Labour chiefs having 'backed out'. Here, they trumpeted, was Sir Tom Cowie, who had done so much for Sunderland; Eric Bramfitt, who had given nearly 40 years' local service; and, last but not least, Jimmy Montgomery, whose superhuman saves had revived the glory days at Roker. Why couldn't they be honoured? The three were to have been the first Freemen of the new

City; Kate Adie and the crew of *HMS Arrow* had been the last Freemen honoured under Sunderland's Borough status. The *Echo* talked of a Council 'gaffe' and personal 'snubs' for three local lads. The next day, the paper followed up with an interview with six local inhabitants of Sunderland. The reaction was almost unanimously favourable: 'A promise is a promise', and 'They've done a lot for the City', were recurring themes, although one woman viewed all such honours as 'a waste of public money'. Sir Tom watched with interest.

The City Tory Leader, Councillor Ron Smith, who served on the Honours Sub-Committee, took up the political cudgels on behalf of all three. 'Think what Tom Cowie has done for this City. Economically, he could have had his headquarters anywhere he liked, but he's stuck with his home town'. Similar indignant protestations were made on Eric and Jimmy's behalf. Eric Bramfitt had given his 40-odd years, and Jimmy Montgomery was 'still working with youngsters in football'. But their protests were in vain: the Council leader cited financial grounds and prudent bookkeeping on behalf of the citizens of Sunderland. The idea behind the awards was merely being deferred, he said; it most certainly did not preclude them being granted 'at some point' in the future.

In spite of this snub, Tom Cowie's loyalty to his City has never wavered. Neither has his patriotism: 'It is too easy to knock Britain and its institutions, but there's nowhere else I would rather live. There was a time when I seriously considered moving abroad—Guernsey, Jersey or the Isle of Man—for tax reasons, as friends like Sir Julian Hodge have done—but I could not have survived in such political backwaters, idyllic though they are. It is Sunderland and its community that have nurtured me from childhood, and that I cannot forget'.

Chapter Twenty Seven

Parting

The year 1992 began well. As Tom Cowie (now Sir Tom), surveyed his business empire, the prospect was pleasing. Cowie Interleasing was the leading vehicle contract-hire operation in the UK, while the motor division boasted 20 dealership locations throughout the country. The bus and coach divisions seemed similarly blessed: Grey-Green was London's top independent operator, with 172 vehicles, servicing 13 bus routes. Over 10 million passengers a year reached their destinations under the provisions of Cowies' London Regional Transport contract.

By early summer, the Group was bidding for Henly's—one of the most respected names in the motor trade. The initial bid involved one new Cowie share for two of Henlys' ordinary shares. Henlys' shares were being valued at 71p, a generous 25–28 per cent up on their quoted price. Nearly 19 million new Cowie shares would be issued if the bid was successful. Cowie's were bidding for the whole Henly's Group, valued at £27 million, and the idea was to combine the two under Cowie control, following the appropriate streamlining and rationalisation.

The offer involved seven new Cowie ordinary shares for every 10 of Henlys', or one new Cowie ordinary share plus 40p for every two of Henlys', representing a 40 per cent increase in capital value. The concern of the Stock Exchange panel that vets such deals related to certain net-assets bar charts, and they asked for clarification on wording and the profit forecasts from Price Waterhouse. It was crucial that all was fully in accord with the requirements of the City Code. 'Despite all our efforts, Henly's were hostile to our bid, and dismissive of our plans. Clever marketing of their interpretation of the facts meant we were never really in a position to challenge the control wielded by the Henly Board. They played a good defensive game, and their handling always appeared more professional than ours. Our bid failed and, while Henlys' shares soared in value, we were well and truly hung out to dry by the financial press, and our shares took an inevitable tumble for the time being. Henly's must rank as the biggest missed opportunity in Cowies' history'.

Sir Tom had agreed to let Gordon Hodgson have a free rein, a move he would later regret. Andrew Cowie had left the group some time before, to become a Name at Lloyds. Hodgson appointed the merchant bankers Noble Grossart to act on Cowies' behalf. Sir Tom believed that the appointment of Noble Grossart had been a mistake; Hodgson disagreed. He called a meeting to discuss the Henly bid and failed to notify Sir Tom— but he miscalculated the loyalty within the Group to the man they still saw as their employer. Before the meeting, Sir Tom was tipped off that it was to take place.

'I turned up unannounced to say my piece, and Gordon's barely suppressed rage hit me with full force. This was a defining moment; I left the meeting knowing in my mind the Henly bid would fail. The rest of the Board seemed confident, but my instincts told me otherwise. I bet Neil Pykett, Iain Jane and Steve Lonsdale about £20 to £25 each, that this was likely to happen, and I took no pleasure in collecting my winnings. That was a truly Pyrrhic victory'.

The inner turmoil over the Henly bid was damaging to the relationship between Sir Tom and Gordon Hodgson. Life went on, and the day-to-day running of the Group continued apace, but a poisoned atmosphere was no place for either man to work to full potential. Colleagues could not speak face to face, but were forced to send notes and memos to adjoining offices. There was countermanding of orders and disagreement even over the colour of the carpet in certain parts of Millfield House—whether it should be 'entrance-hall green' or 'executive blue' outside the office of a director's secretary. Something had to give.

'My last 12 months of active participation at Cowies were a sad end to a glorious journey. Gordon Hodgson and myself had been a superb team at times over the years but, as he increasingly found it impossible to speak directly to me, how could I give what I believed to be helpful advice? On at least one occasion I was told that he tore a strip off a member of staff who had my picture adorning his office wall. I'd seen myself easing into a position as a non-executive Chairman, essentially in a guiding and advisory capacity. It was not to be'.

Meanwhile, the acquisitions continued and, in December, Cowie's bought Foster Cars Ltd (a motor dealership trading in Wakefield), for £950,000 cash. They also acquired Lexus and Toyota franchises, another small link in the chain. On 28 May 1993, the Cowie Group announced its intention to acquire Keep Trust Ltd, and 13,972,956 new Cowie ordinary shares were duly issued at 212p to raise the £28.6 million needed.

Keep Trust operated 18 dealerships in England and Wales, encompassing Vauxhall, Ford, Rover, Nissan, Toyota and Peugeot, plus Iveco Ford commercial-vehicle dealerships and a Kawasaki motor-cycle franchise. By now, using the services of N. M. Rothschild and Son Ltd, Cowie's had laid out a careful strategy, emphasising their proven record. This bid was received favourably by Keep Trust's directors (who included Tony O'Reilly, the Irish business tycoon), but lessons had been learned from the Henly's débâcle: Cowie's were taking no chances on there being any possible misinterpretations or misunderstandings.

Again, it was Gordon Hodgson who handled the Keep Trust bid. Keep Trust was essentially a hotchpotch of dealerships—substantial, certainly, but scarcely with the kudos that Henly's had possessed. Tom Cowie was acutely aware of being kept out of things, though in a polite fashion: 'I felt any assistance I could offer would thereafter be received with a mixture of suspicion and contempt. The Chairman was being inexorably isolated at Board level and beyond. At a full Board meeting, I recognised things were far from what they should be, and volunteered to stand down if I had outstayed my welcome. I had full knowledge of what had been going on, but there seemed little point in fighting it. To do so would truly have portrayed me as a sad, old dinosaur, not to mention the "megalomaniac" to which I was later likened in the *Financial Times*'.

It was decided that Sir Tom would go by the end of 1993. His future position with the Company would be purely nominal, though held for life. After 45 years he felt that he was being put out to grass. 'At least I would go with dignity. There were those who regretted seeing me depart, but the decision was taken. I'm quite sure none of them envisaged the power struggles that would follow. Iain Jane was the Board's appointed spokesman, bringing the expected verdict. Ironic really, as he was ousted a little over a year later. My PA, Maureen Bryant, was informed that she no longer had a job with the Group.

She cleared her desk on 17 August 1993; I'd done so a week before. The option to stay until 31 December 1993 seemed meaningless, not to mention masochistic. At least I had the grouse-shooting to look forward to, and striding the moors among friends. The leaving was a wrench, but scarcely a shock. I'd been preparing for this in terms of my business papers and so forth for some time but, even so there was a last-minute rush and lots of overly fast decisions to be made as to what to take and what to dispose of.

Boxes and files were dispatched to Broadwood Hall, some of them largely untouched to this day. It's odd, seeing a life's work reduced to a series of cardboard containers. All the happy memories; all the loyal friends, staff and business acquaintances who will no longer figure in your daily life. It was a painful parting'.

No doubt, Hodgson saw Tom Cowie in a less-than-flattering light. It could have been galling to see someone who so obviously enjoyed the trappings of wealth, who knew how to delegate and fill the leisure time he now enjoyed. In addition, there was the award of the OBE, the title, the Fellowship of the Chartered Institute of Transport and the Freedom of the City of London. Easy to see why a sense of the injustice of things might blossom. Hodgson was wealthy now, but it was Tom who dined with the good and great, wore custom-made shirts from Turnbull and Asser, strode the grouse moors and generally lived like a lord—yet retained his bond with the workforce and was equally at ease on the shop-floor. It was a balancing act Hodgson might have envied. That Tom took time off to indulge his pastimes was a source of conflict (and perhaps that sense of injustice had some basis in fact), but it would have been better if such grievances had been thoroughly discussed and an attempt made to resolve them.

Today, over a decade on, Sir Tom displays little venom towards Hodgson, although he cheerfully admits a temptation to take him by the throat at the time. 'As a business man I would rate him five star. People warned me about him, but he was delivering the goods and I rewarded him accordingly. I think he grew tired of living in my shadow and perhaps I was too healthy ... it may be that he grew tired of waiting for me to decline. Those directors who were persuaded to turn against me didn't last long: Lord Elliott of Morpeth was the only one who stayed faithful, and he paid the price. I suspect my title made the rift between myself and Gordon Hodgson even wider, although I felt his part in the Cowie Group's advancement had been vital. Perhaps my acknowledging his undeniable worth added to the problem. I guess he just could not accept the Company could never be his in the way it had been mine. In his eyes, I got all the adulation while he did what he felt was the bulk of the work, but it was I who started and built the Company up to the modern giant it was as the 1990s dawned'. That giant employed 3,676 people and was worth £403.5 million when Cowie was ousted.

Afterwards, employees were too scared to speak to the former Chairman. His picture was taken down from the wall and, if he telephoned any of his former colleagues, it had to be in secret. Now Sir Tom sees Hodgson as '...my biggest disappointment. I made him a wealthy man and in the end I lost control of the Company I had given my life to building'.

SIR TOM COWIE

Chapter Twenty Eight

The Moors

The pain of separation from the company he had built was deep and lasting. Tom Cowie had taken Cowie's from a back-street operation to a mighty corporation—and now he was out on his ear. What made it worse was that the man who had ousted him was someone he had raised to the pinnacle of power—the same man who now seemed determined to rub salt into the wound.

'I was barely out of the front door at Millfield House when Gordon had the "T. Cowie PLC" name-plate altered to "Cowie Group PLC". Unfortunately for him, the Cowie name remained over the entrance as a constant reminder. I had a fair old struggle, over the ensuing months, to obtain even my office desk and table from Millfield House. For sentimental reasons, I wanted to use them at the Broadwood Hall office. They had "gone missing", but were eventually located in a remote storeroom, the table minus one of its legs and rather the worse for wear. What an unseemly mess, and so unnecessary'.

Deprived of his office in Cowies' headquarters, Sir Tom was forced to operate from his family dining-table while arrangements were put in hand to convert the stables at Broadwood Hall into an office block. Later on, the man who had founded the Company would not even receive a Company diary or a Company turkey at Christmas.

'What had happened to me must have come as a massive shock to most of the staff at Cowie's, especially those not at Millfield House. They had been aware there was an atmosphere ... the blazing rows were scarcely conducted in polite silence ... but nevertheless it was a surprise to the troops. I received a wealth of supportive phone calls and letters, which must have been irksome to some but were balm to me'.

The Cowie name remained over the entrance for four years and then Hodgson acted: on 6 November 1997, a specially convened shareholders' meeting voted to change the Company name to 'ARRIVA'. It was supposedly deemed 'more appropriate for the planned European expansion of Cowie's as an international car and bus company'. The change did not please Sir Tom.

'For the princely sum of £100,000, image consultants came up with this piece of Euro-friendly mellifluence, after testing 450 possibilities in 15 different countries. A further £1.5 million was lashed out on the repainting. For me, it smacked of extreme personal animosity rather than sound business acumen'. 'Cowie is not a pretty word', pronounced one executive, while Gordon Hodgson proclaimed that 'ARRIVA gives promise and reassurance to our customers'.

It is possible that the Board were stung by Sir Tom's attacks on them. He accused them of megalomania when they sacked director Neil Pykett, commenting 'I ran a very happy ship and there was none of this rubbish going on'. On the day that the Cowie name was axed, the then Chairman, Sir James McKinnon, wrote to Sir Tom to inform him that his Life Presidency was removed. The suggestion was that, by criticising the Board, he was acting against the best interests of the company. Perhaps this was true; it is equally possible that the action gave some people personal satisfaction.

Sir Tom still speaks charitably of the man who ousted him: 'Gordon promoted a policy of spreading the Group's ownership of bus companies across the country, and for this he is to be applauded'. Nevertheless, however much he may downplay it, there is no doubt that his ousting from the company he had built almost broke Tom Cowie's heart.

Four years after Sir Tom's departure, Gordon Hodgson stepped down from the Chairmanship. It was as though, once he had achieved his aim of stepping from under Tom Cowie's shadow, he was content to let go—however, not before he had got rid of most of the Board members who had backed his move to wrest the company from its founder. It is ironic that those same members might well have retained their positions if Sir

Tom had continued in office. Gordon Hodgson was asked to give his version of his time at Cowie's and his battle with Sir Tom, but declined to contribute to this book.

After the débâcle at Cowie's, Sir Tom sought refuge in what had been only a hobby while he was still with the company. He had been over 40 years of age when his interest in shooting began, at first using a borrowed gun and accompanying two of his employees on a rough shoot. Soon, he found that he was a good shot—even an excellent one—and what had begun as a diversion became an absorption. He openly declares that to keep a grouse moor was lunatic, and yet he revelled in the difficulties. He is at his happiest at a shooting party and has never been known to quit, however bad the conditions. Grouse are his favourite pursuit because they are a challenge—the trickiest of quarries—going from 0 to 70 mph as they try to escape. He does not mind that he may stand for an hour in the cold and never see a bird because, at any moment, the sky may suddenly be dark with them. But he likes to win: in this, as in business, the Cowie bag must be the best.

'My interest in grouse-shooting has developed gradually over 30 to 40 years. I shot rabbits alongside father with a 2.2 rifle as a lad, and in my 40s got involved with the odd little "rough shoot", running my own syndicate. In 1989, I was to do a deal with the executors of the late Lord Strathmore, taking out a 14-year lease on probably the best grouse moors in Europe—maybe even the world. He was a close personal friend, with a seat on Cowies' Board until his sudden, untimely death at the age of 57. For a time I shared the tenancy with the late Sir Joseph Nickerson, shooting predominantly at Wemmergill in County Durham, where the average yield is 2809 brace.

Sir Tom's acquaintance with the 17th Earl of Strathmore began on the moors, but became a close personal friendship. Ask Sir Tom about Fergie Strathmore's funeral at Glamis and a sadness falls upon him. It was there, standing near to the Queen mourning her uncle, that he suddenly realised how far he had travelled from Westbury Street—but there was no exultation in the fact, for he was mourning a friend.

Shooting is a love, a passion, a full-time commitment—especially when the "Glorious Twelfth" arrives. Even the timing of family weddings has to take that into account. Having failed to get me interested in golf, Edgar Turner tried valiantly to interest me in salmon fishing—"Something for you to do in those other six months of the year"—but to no avail'.

Managing a grouse-shooting moor requires both administrative and environmental skills and the help of experienced keepers. He also has a hard-working office staff—among them Maureen Bryant, who has been his loyal PA for most of the last 46 years, both at Cowie's and subsequently at his Broadwood Hall Estate Office.

From heather-burning to the upkeep of the buildings; from predator control to the organising of shoots for an international (and sometimes royal) clientele; he can combine business with pleasure and indulge his natural inclination to be busy and productive. But if his prowess on the moors is legendary, so is his determination to get his own way, whatever it takes. It is a legend in shooting circles that, on one occasion, deprived of the peg he wanted, he hired the whole pheasant shoot and spent a day there, a single gun, shooting where he pleased. The story is apocryphal, perpetuated by a columnist who should have known better. It probably sprang from his taking an occasional 250 bird day for himself, simply to enjoy his sport.

At 80 plus, his schedule for the season would make many a 40-year-old wilt. Grouse are his favourite sport because they are fast-flying and difficult, but shooting has taken him all over the world. A cherished companion in Africa and South America is the best-selling novelist, Wilbur Smith, who well remembers their first meeting at Heathrow Airport in 1993: 'We were off to shoot partridges with Tom Gullick in Spain. We took to one another at once and laughed all the way there and all the way back'.

Wilbur Smith is a frequent visitor to Murton Grange (Sir Tom's shoot in North Yorkshire, arguably the best pheasant shoot in England), as is the opera star, Dame Kiri Te Kanawa, to whom Tom was introduced by another shooting friend, racing driver Jackie Stewart. Together, Sir Tom and Wilbur Smith have shot doves in Cordoba, Argentina, and wild guinea-fowl and wild doves in Zambia and Zimbabwe. His shooting schedule for 2004 shows that he is as active as ever, sometimes out every day during shooting weeks. In addition to Murton Grange, he also has a shoot at Ruffside, a village he owns near Edmundbyers in County Durham.

He loves the cold and rigour of the shoot but equally relishes the dinner-parties, where his wife, Diana, is an excellent hostess and the conversation sparkles. It pleases him, too, that on the moors and round the dinner-table his guests and his family mingle, for his children and their partners are keen on the sport. Engrossing as the moors might be, however, Tom Cowie was too much the entrepreneur to give up wheeling and dealing altogether; he needed another challenge.

SIR TOM COWIE

Chapter Twenty Nine

NEMS

In 1989, Captain Nick Barker established a small business on the banks of the Wear. He had enjoyed a distinguished naval career that had culminated in the command of *HMS Endurance*, patrolling the waters around the Falklands. He repeatedly warned the British Government of the likely consequences of ignoring the increasingly bellicose attitude of the Argentinians. His fears were dismissed, but history was to prove him right within a very short space of time. A Devonian by birth, he came to Sunderland on his retirement from the Royal Navy. He had visited the port often when in command of *HMS Arrow* and *HMS Endurance* (both Sunderlandsponsored ships), and had found the port authorities and the local council co-operative. His ambition was to found a company called the Sea Safety Centre, acting as an agent for marine suppliers of life-rafts and the like. He took on staff and opened in ramshackle premises, his logo a giant penguin he had photographed during his time in the South Atlantic. Alas, the agencies he had been promised failed to materialise! He dabbled in ships' supplies – Cola at seven pence a can, and the like – but the staff he had taken on needed to be paid and his financial position was soon precarious.

Now Charles Bucknall came on the scene. He had left the Army in 1987, but his first venture—a helicopter company in Saudi Arabia—was scuppered by the Gulf War. Back in England, he worked in the City, dealing in futures, but his real desire was to move to the north-east of England where he had family connections. He became increasingly intrigued by stories of the glut of metal pouring out of the former Iron Curtain countries, and his City experience showed that trading in metal was lucrative. An accidental meeting with Nick Barker was a catalyst: Barker had warehousing and a failing business; Bucknall had ambition and knowledge, and together they fought to keep the Barker enterprise afloat. Bucknall managed to get the warehouse registered with the London Metal Exchange—a prerequisite for dealing—and the first metal was shipped in through the Port of Sunderland in 1993.

For a while, metal importing co-existed with the ships' chandlery but, increasingly, Bucknall fretted over Barker's opposition to streamlining the business or paying-off any of the employees. Margaret, the bookkeeper, who operated from a shabby, smoke-filled caravan parked inside the warehouse, uttered dire warnings about cash flow, but Barker remained intransigent: years of command had instilled in him total loyalty to his men or women; no one would be paid off; something would turn up. Bucknall, with a wife and two young children to support, was less sanguine. Together, they worked in a windowless office and, to add to his problems, the other half of the warehouse (once occupied by a shot-blasting company), was an empty shell having been destroyed by fire two years before.

Eventually, things came to a head. Without an infusion of cash they would have to cease trading, and Barker came up with a suggestion: Tom Cowie was an occasional shooting acquaintance; perhaps he could be persuaded to step in until the promised 'killings' in the metal market materialised. To this end, they prepared an optimistic report on the Sea Safety Centre and arranged a meeting. Charles Bucknall remembers that meeting well: it took place in Nick Barker's flat in the Jungle—a seamens' dive on the fish quay in North Shields which had been turned into smart apartments overlooking the Tyne.

Bucknall's heart was in his mouth, for he knew the true state of the business. Barker intended to ask Cowie to stand as a guarantor; if that failed, he would sell him 30 per cent of the equity. Within minutes, Cowie had cut through the waffle of the report and laid bare the financial facts. While the two men held their breath, he cogitated and then made them an offer. There would be no guarantee and no 30 per cent: 'I can't get to grips with being a minority shareholder'. That he needed control was apparent to both Barker and Bucknall. If they gave him that control he would invest in their company and set it on its feet. Barker was dubious but, to Bucknall, Tom Cowie appeared an exciting figure. He also looked like a saviour—someone who had grasped the potential of the metals business. Perhaps Cowie saw the cash potential of metal importing; more likely, he saw its impact on his birthplace. As he was leaving, he said, 'Everything is leaving Sunderland. Once, four million tons of coal were shipped out of that port. I want to see it humming again'.

Sir Tom remembers the meeting, too. 'Profits were optimistically glimpsed in the distance, but in essence this jaunty wing-and-a-prayer operation was more likely to rub shoulders with bankruptcy before long. What was needed, amongst other things, was a substantial cash injection, and I was more than reluctant to get involved at first. But Nick was very nice and wonderfully persuasive, and I began to ponder the possibilities that the business, with all its trading contacts, represented. I eventually invested a lot of money and built up a substantial stake, about 95 per cent. After August 1995 I began analysing the business in detail and proceeded to discard most operational aspects in order to concentrate on the metal importation'.

At first, monthly accounts were necessary, and Sir Tom brought in his stepdaughter, Kate (a qualified accountant) to help. The firm had faced tax losses of £1.5 million but eventually Sir Tom and Charles Bucknall turned it around, together with Colin Wilson, an accountant who joined the firm—which by now was called North European Marine Services Ltd (NEMS)—in 1996. They subsequently purchased a property company to supply the necessary extra space for

NEMS—over 300,000 square feet of warehousing, all Sunderland based, and embracing parts of both the dock area and the City itself. To Bucknall's relief, he now has an office with a window and a magnificent view of the port. Much of the NEMS property is situated on the banks of the Wear, near to the Port of Sunderland. Sir Tom was astonished to find, while examining the deeds, that his new enterprise is built on the very spot where his grandparents' house in North Moor Street once stood—the house he visited as a child.

Sir Tom's enthusiasm has grown with the company. 'Bitten by the metal bug, I've since started another company, Penguin Metals, whereby we buy metal by the 1,000 tons and sell it off in 50–100-ton lots. The synergistic value of this enterprise when linked to NEMS is obvious: use of NEMS' warehouses means that we don't have to pay rent to someone else, and I have, to hand, a workforce complete with fork-lift trucks to handle the merchandise'. The pattern is there to see—a mixture of luck, common sense and the nerve to grasp the moment that has been his trademark. His one regret is that he did not come to metal trading sooner. 'If I'd started out in this business, all other things being equal, I reckon I could have made it extremely profitable, for the opportunities are many. Those with a lifetime in this sector rank amongst the wealthiest in the land. Russia possesses vast opportunities for visionaries armed with venture capital, China likewise. I visited Lithuania a few years ago and was staggered by the near-medieval nature of both farming and industry there. When the Iron Curtain was lifted it exposed a system ripe for enterprise. The Western nations need to move swiftly if corruption is not to overtake the emerging Eastern bloc states with a totality equalling anything Lenin or Stalin imposed'.

Sir Tom has always been ready to travel on NEMS' behalf, and Bucknall admires his shrewdness and his capacity to take in the minutiae of a deal. Once, meeting in an airport with one of the biggest Russian metal-trading companies, Sir Tom encountered his good friend, motor-racing celebrity Jackie Stewart and introduced him to the Russians. Suitably impressed, they concluded the deal in record time. Bucknall describes it as a surreal experience, but one he obviously enjoyed. Today, the Company has moved on, expanded its operations and broadened its outlook. Now part of a Group Company called Sir Tom Cowie Holdings Limited, the Group encompasses UK warehouse operations in Sunderland, Newcastle, Hull and Liverpool, with around 650,000 square feet of bonded warehouse space; warehousing in the region of 100,000 tons of aluminium, copper and zinc; as well as bonded wines and spirits, and document and furniture storage. It also has a metal-trading company that specialises in the sales of zinc and aluminium to UK industry; a property company that owns warehousing and light-industrial property, as well as residential property developments; and, finally, a car dealership that was set up in 2003 – somewhat ironic, when ARRIVA have come out of the retail motor trade. Abroad, the group has warehouses storing tin, indium and zinc, as well as other metals, in Singapore. There are operations in North and South China, Taiwan and Malaysia; and the group is actively involved in shipping and supervising metal movement throughout the world. NEMS is a rapidly expanding business which, one day, may assume the gigantic proportions of Tom Cowie's original venture.

Chapter Thirty

Fulfilment

In 1989, Tom Cowie became Chairman of the Wearside Partnership—a 'compact between education, industry and the community'. The Partnership is concerned with primary, secondary and special-needs schools, and these schools made a profound impression on him. 'In institutions such as the Barbara Priestman School, where a lot of the kids are in wheelchairs, the joy of living is palpable. At the various schools for the disadvantaged ... drugs, split families, poverty ... pupils interact with teachers who genuinely care about them'.

It grieves him that some of the children get depressed when the summer holidays approach and they have to stay at home—something other children would revel in. He has given hundreds of thousands of pounds to the children of Sunderland over the years. The *Sunday Times* Rich List for 2003 said that he 'has turned his back on a lifetime of earning money and is giving it away instead. His name has become a byword for charity in the Sunderland area. In the past year, Sunderland University has benefited to the tune of more than £400,000 ... he has given away almost £1 million in the past 12 months'.

In fact, £400,000 is only a small part of Sir Tom's contribution to the University. His involvement in its expansion dates from 1992, when he was given an Honorary Doctorate of Business Administration. Since then, he has involved himself in all aspects of university life and he has formed an excellent working partnership with the Vice-Chancellor, Peter Fidler, who values Sir Tom's contribution to the life of the campus: 'Time and again I have watched his genuine delight as he chats to students, quizzing them vigorously about the University and their achievements and ambitions. In years gone by, many of them would have had no hope of higher education – not because they weren't clever enough, but because of where they came from and their family circumstances – because university 'wasn't for the likes of us'. Sir Tom has helped to create a much better future for young people in Sunderland – one in which their horizons are wider and their aims higher'.

Sunderland is a fast-developing modern university. The Research Assessment Exercise in 2001 rated Sunderland as the best 'new' university in the country for the overall quality, range and quantity of its research. Many of its buildings have been constructed on reclaimed land formerly used by the old heavy-industry sector. From the ruin of the old, phoenix-like, has come a revival: the new campus is quite magnificent, rising along the River Wear and around St Peter's Church, which dates from AD 674. In 2002 the campus, formerly called St Peter's, was renamed the Sir Tom Cowie Campus at St Peter's, in recognition of his longstanding, loyal support for the University. Lord Puttnam, the University Chancellor, declared himself 'hugely grateful for all he continues to do for the University, the City and the region', and the Education Secretary, Estelle Morris, paid him special tribute. Peter Fidler is also grateful for Sir Tom's contribution: 'Sir Tom wants the best for Sunderland and for all its young people. He left school early to make his own way in the world – hugely successfully – and I'm sure he would be the first to say that people should take responsibility for their own lives. But he also recognises that, today, education is the key to individual self-improvement as well as the economic revival of our region. The Government's performance indicators show we are one of the very best universities in the country for widening participation in higher education. The same statistics also show our graduates are highly employable – 93 per cent of them are in employment or further training within six months of qualifying. Our "hatcheries" are now growing new businesses from amongst our enterprising students and graduates. The University continues to welcome an increasing international community of new students and project partners as our reputation grows. The facilities that Sir Tom has helped us to create, underpin all these achievements.'

His generosity to the University is well known, and appreciated. Less well known, but just as welcome, are the numerous smaller benefactions – a church roof here; a gift to a sports club there; £50,000 to establish a 1920s garage at Beamish, the industrial-heritage museum; another £50,000 to preserve the history of Sunderland. Each year there is a Christmas outing for children in care; he has donated £50,000 to establish a specialist maths and computing school at Southmoor; another £50,000 for a business and enterprise college at Thornhill; and £12,500 to win specialist technology status for Hetton School. The list of his gifts is almost endless. With each gift, Sir Tom is shoring up the fabric of his City and its environs. This concern for others had manifested itself early on. Jack Keerie, who worked at Cowie's all his life – the same Jack Keerie who braved the snow in Lanchester – tells this story: 'One day the boss said: "That old chap who lives in the cottage near me is in trouble. Go and see if we can help him". I visited the cottage and found the owner eked out a living making fence-posts. His business was at a standstill because his form of power had its engine burned out. Parts for it were unobtainable because it was a Peters engine the old man had acquired when his father was a fitter in the Royal Corps in the First World War. I got another engine, had it overhauled and installed it for him. I reported to the boss that I had carried out his instructions. Every so often after that he would ask me if I had been to see the old man and was everything all right'.

Another of Sir Tom's ventures is a 1,400-acre farm in North Yorkshire, near Rievaulx Abbey. 'It's extremely time consuming, but thankfully I have an excellent farmer managing it for me. He farms the property next to mine and is available to do contract work as and when I need it. I cannot but admire his sheer energy and undoubted expertise. We're essentially an arable farm, growing wheat, barley and oil-seed rape—a typical mix of fuel and food crops (though oil-seed rape is one of the banes of my life at Broadwood Hall, filling many of the nearby fields and irritating my hay fever into bouts of coughs and splutters). The farm isn't an organic concern as yet, though I can see the benefits of going down that path, both in environmental terms and because consumers are increasingly demanding these more naturally grown products. You ignore your potential customers at your peril'. Motor-bikes or farming—he still respects the customer.

His family are a joy to him, scattered though they now are. His son, Andrew, lives at Ruffside. The four daughters of his marriage to Lillas—Elizabeth, Susan, Sarah and Emma—are all married and live in southern England. Alex, the eldest child of his marriage to Diana, married in June 2003 and works in property development. Charlotte lives in London and works worldwide for an international publishing company, while Victoria is a keen horsewoman and spends most of her time eventing at a reasonably high level. Kate, Sir Tom's stepdaughter, lives in North Yorkshire and has returned to work as an accountant after the birth of her second child. Steven, her brother, lives in London, where he is working in technological development. Sir Tom has nine grandchildren and three great-grandchildren.

Each year, the whole family gathers at the resort of Chewton Glen in Hampshire. He revels in seeing his large family together and the closeness between them. Sir Tom and Lady Diana have spent the worst of the winter in Barbados for the last 25 years; they love the Barbadian climate and have many expatriate friends there. They holiday, too, with his sister, Emma, at her home in Spain or cruising. He is, he constantly maintains, a very lucky man: his family are healthy and successful; his metal-importing business goes from strength to strength; his farm prospers; and, as Chairman of the Development Trust, he has raised £10 million for the University of Sunderland Media and Arts Centre on the banks of the River Wear, which opened in June 2003.

Today, ARRIVA is one of Britain's leading companies. The business that sprang from the determination of a young ex-serviceman, battling the effects of a painful bowel condition and the shortages of post-war Britain, has become one of the largest enterprises in the country, employing 32,000 people and worth £757 million. In April 2001, his Life Presidency of ARRIVA was restored to him and he now enjoys an excellent relationship with its chief executive, Bob Davies, a man he much admires.

Most men, faced with a 'palace coup' as he was in 1993, would have retreated to their grouse moors and their charitable causes. Not Tom Cowie: still looking for a ladder to ascend, he took on NEMS and has turned it from a failing company to the thriving business it is today. He has been honoured by the Queen, but the affection of his fellow citizens means as much. When a group of Sunderland people thronging the Market Square were asked what they knew of Tom Cowie, they all knew who he was: most referred to his gifts to schools and to the University; others spoke of his provision of employment over the years; one old lady summed him up thus: 'Tommy Cowie? He's a canny lad!'.

His character is complicated. Ruthless in business dealing, he can be magnanimous in defeat, as his refusal to condemn Gordon Hodgson outright reveals. He is equally at home among the rich and famous or with his fellow citizens as they live their everyday lives. He does not like losing or coming second, in the boardroom or in the sporting field, but he does not harbour grudges. Nor has his encounter with ingratitude in business or in the Council Chamber made him lose trust in people or withdraw his generosity. His anger is quick—he confesses to thrashing parcels that defy opening—but it subsides as quickly as it arises. He is, in other words, a very human being, fallible yet indomitable, a man who has made his mark upon his City and his time.

In 1994 he gave the University over £600,000 to build a lecture theatre. At its inauguration, the then Vice-Chancellor, Ann Wright, asked: 'What better example could there be for our students than the story of a Sunderland man who started out of a small shop selling motor-bikes with a capital of £1,000 and over 40 years built one of the fastest-growing motor-sales and financial concerns in Europe? In the light of such success some people would lose sight of their origins but Sir Tom is, and always will be, a Sunderland man'.

A new title now adorns the huge warehouses above the Wear, which house part of his operations – Sir Tom Cowie Holdings Ltd. The Cowie name is back where it belongs.

SIR TOM COWIE